Contents

Age-Appropriate Skills

Language

- following directions
- story comprehension
- descriptive and comparative language
- rhyming
- categorization
- letter and sound recognition
- statements and questions
- auditory and visual memory
- left to right tracking
- oral language
- vocabulary and concept development
- sequencing
- color words

Math

- counting to 20
- patterning
- numeral recognition
- geometric shapes
- ordinal numbers
- beginning computation
- one-to-one matching
- graphing
- measurement

Circle-Time Books

 Making Circle-Time Books ....

Use these simple directions to assemble a circle-time book for each of the five sections of *The Rainforest*.

- Tear out and laminate the color story pages for each circle-time book.

- Bind the books with binder rings or an alternative binding method.

- Read the circle-time book as the opening activity for each section of *The Rainforest*.

Place the book on an easel or chalkboard stand and flip the pages for easy reading.

 Sharing Circle-Time Books ....

Each circle-time story introduces the topic of that section. Begin by reading the story to the children several times. The first time you read it, you might ask children to predict what the story will be about by looking at the cover illustration. In subsequent readings, use strategies such as:

- moving your finger under words as you read to model left to right tracking

- allowing children to "read" the predictable text

- asking children to identify objects in the pictures

- talking about any rhyming words

- asking children to predict what will happen next in the story

- asking questions to help children recall story details

- asking at least one question that relates to children's own lives

Circle-Time Books

Section One
Walk in the Rainforest

"Walk in the Rainforest" (pages 13–22)
This book uses rhythm and rhyme to introduce children to the rainforest unit of study. Before reading, ask the children if they know what a rainforest is. What do they think they would find there? Pause on each page and discuss the illustrations and rhyming words. Explain to the children that during the rainforest unit they will be learning more about the rainforest and the plants, animals, and people who live there.

Ask questions such as:
- What are the trees like in the rainforest?
- Does it rain all the time?
- What grows in the rainforest?
- Who lives in the rainforest?
- What might you hear on a walk through the rainforest?
- Can you make some animal sounds?

Section Two
Up into the Rainforest

"Up into the Rainforest" (pages 51–60)
This book uses humor to introduce the concept that the rainforest has layers (forest floor, understory, canopy, and emergent). It also describes an animal that lives in each layer, from the tiny ant to the powerful harpy eagle. On a second reading, have the children join in the refrain, "I am king of the rainforest."

Ask questions such as:
- In which part of the rainforest does the ant live?
- In which part of the rainforest does the bat live?
- In which part of the rainforest does the spider monkey live?
- Who is king of the rainforest?
- In which part of the rainforest does the harpy eagle live?

Section Three
Plants, Plants, Plants

"Plants, Plants, Plants" (pages 91–100)
This story uses repetitive language to introduce children to some of the characteristics of rainforest plants. Discuss trees over 100 feet tall, large buttress roots above ground, flowers that bloom at night, flowers pollinated by specialized bees that only visit one type of flower, plants that grow on trees and without roots, and plants that trap insects. The rainforests are ancient forests.

Ask questions such as:
- Which are the tallest plants in the rainforest?
- What holds up the tall trees?
- When do some flowers bloom?
- Where do some plants grow?

Circle-Time Books

"Rainforest Animals" (pages 127–136)
This story uses descriptive language to familiarize children with some of the animals of the rainforest. During repeated readings, invite the children to use movements that imitate the behavior of each animal.

Ask questions such as:

- Which word describes a hummingbird?
- Which word describes the teeth of the piranha?
- Which word describes the tree frog's feet?
- Which word describes the capybara? The butterfly? The toucan? The anaconda? The jaguar?
- What does the toucan like to eat?
- What do you think the jaguar is watching?

"Rainforest Family" (pages 163–172)
Through repetitive language, this story introduces children to a family native to the rainforest. Explain to the children that some families in the rainforest have modern conveniences such as motorboats, Jet Skis®, radios, and TVs. However, many families garden, hunt, and make tools. Tell the children to listen for things that the rainforest provides as you read the story aloud.

Ask questions such as:

- What are some of the things that keep people busy in the rainforest?
- What kind of pet do the children in the story have? Would you like to have a pet monkey?
- What is their home made of? What is your home made of?

Take-Home Books

Use these simple directions to make reproducible take-home books for each of the five sections of *The Rainforest*.

1. Reproduce the book pages for each child.
2. Cut the pages along the cut lines.
3. Place the pages in order, or this may be done as a sequencing activity with children. Guide children in assembling the book page by page.
4. Staple the book together.

After making each take-home book, review the story as children turn the pages of their own books. Send the storybook home along with the Parent Letter on page 5.

Dear Parent(s) or Guardian(s),

As part of our unit *The Rainforest*, I will be presenting five storybooks to the class. Your child will receive a take-home storybook for you to share. Remember that reading to children helps them develop a love of reading. Regularly reading aloud to children has proven to enhance a variety of early language skills, including:

- vocabulary and concept development,
- letter recognition,
- phonemic awareness,
- auditory and visual discrimination, and
- left to right tracking.

I hope you enjoy sharing these stories with your child.

As you read to your child, remember to:

1. speak clearly and with interest.
2. track words by moving your finger under each word as you read it.
3. ask your child to help you identify objects in the pictures. Talk about these objects together.
4. discuss your own experiences as they relate to the story.
5. allow your child to express his or her own thoughts and ideas and to ask you questions.

I hope you enjoy all five of these stories.

Sincerely,

_____

Storyboards

A storyboard is an excellent way to enhance vocabulary and concept development.

Each section of *The Rainforest* includes full-color storyboard pieces to use in extending the language and concepts introduced. Ideas for using the storyboard pieces in each section are found on pages 7–9.

Turn the full-color cutouts into pieces that will adhere to a flannel- or felt-covered storyboard. Just laminate the pieces and affix self-sticking Velcro® dots to the back of each piece.

Walk in the Rainforest
pages 29–33

Up into the Rainforest
pages 67 and 69

Plants, Plants, Plants
pages 107 and 109

Rainforest Animals
pages 143–147

Rainforest Family
pages 179 and 181

Storyboards

"Walk in the Rainforest" Storyboard Use the colorful storyboard pieces on pages 29–33 to follow up your presentation of the story "Walk in the Rainforest." You may choose to use the following teacher script to present the story:

Let's take a walk in the rainforest together! The children are taking a walk. They are going to explore the rainforest with us. It's raining, so the children will use a big leaf for an umbrella. When the sun comes out, it shines on the treetops. We will see brightly colored flowers on our walk. There are lots of green plants, too. Will we get to meet some of the people who live in the rainforest? Greet them with a friendly hello. Keep walking; look around you. Can you tell who else lives in the rainforest? That's right—lots of animals. Can you name some of them?

Remove the storyboard pieces and allow children to replace each piece as they retell the story.

"Up into the Rainforest" Storyboard Use the colorful storyboard pieces on pages 67 and 69 to follow up your presentation of the story "Up into the Rainforest." You may choose to use the following teacher script to present the story:

In our story "Up into the Rainforest," each creature lives in a different part of the rainforest. We call each part a layer of the rainforest. Here is the forest floor. The ant lives on the forest floor. He thinks he is king of the rainforest! Here is the understory, where there are small trees. The bat lives in the understory. He thinks he is king of the rainforest! The next layer is the canopy, where tall trees make a green forest umbrella. The spider monkey lives here. He thinks he is king of the rainforest! The very top layer is the emergent, where a few of the tallest trees poke above the umbrella. The powerful harpy eagle lives here. Do you think he could be king of the rainforest?

Remove the storyboard pieces and allow children to replace each piece as they retell the story.

Storyboards

Section Three
Plants, Plants, Plants

"Plants, Plants, Plants" Storyboard Use the colorful storyboard pieces on pages 107 and 109 to follow up your presentation of the story "Plants, Plants, Plants." You may choose to use the following teacher script to present the story:

Many different kinds of plants grow in the Earth's rainforests. Rainforests have millions of plants. Possibly half the plants that grow on Earth are in the rainforests. Each rainforest has different kinds of plants. Which ones are the tallest? The trees are. Some grow to more than 100 feet tall. They have very big roots to help hold them up. Bats like plants that open up at night the most. Bees love colorful flowers. Some bees go to only one kind of flower, and leave the other ones alone. Here is a bromeliad plant. These plants grow without touching the ground. They like to grow on tree branches. They are sometimes called air plants. Here is a pitcher plant. It opens up like a pitcher. Can you guess what it can trap inside? Bugs! Rainforests have grown for many, many years. Some are as old as the dinosaurs.

Remove the storyboard pieces and allow children to replace each piece as they retell the story.

Section Four
Rainforest Animals

"Rainforest Animals" Storyboard Use the colorful storyboard pieces on pages 143–147 to follow up your presentation of the story "Rainforest Animals." You may choose to use the following teacher script to present the story:

Here are the rainforest trees, and here is a river in the rainforest. Let's find out what kinds of animals live here. Can you help me call them? Let's try. Come out, little hummingbird. (children repeat) Here is the hummingbird. Come out, hungry piranha. (children repeat) Here is the piranha. Can you call the tree frog? (Children: Come out, tree frog.) Here is the tree frog. Can you call the fat capybara? The pretty butterfly? The busy toucan? The big anaconda? The fast jaguar?

Remove the storyboard pieces and allow children to replace each piece as they retell the story.

Storyboards

"Rainforest Family" Storyboard Use the colorful storyboard pieces on pages 179 and 181 to follow up your presentation of the story "Rainforest Family." You may choose to use the following teacher script to present the story:

Here is a village in the rainforest. Let's find out who lives there. Here is the house where a family lives. The house is made from trees. Here are the father and son. They are going hunting today in the rainforest. They will look for food. Here are the mother and daughter. They will have a busy day, too. First, they will collect some nuts. Then, they will work in the garden. Here is the garden where the family grows some of their food. When the work is done, the children will have fun playing with their pet—a monkey! Here is a scene from a typical day for this rainforest tribe.

Remove the storyboard pieces and allow children to replace each piece as they retell the story.

Creating an Atmosphere

Create a delightful rainforest environment in your classroom. Make a bulletin board that displays rainforest-related pictures and information. Hang "vines" from the ceiling. Use a large woven basket to display books about the rainforest.

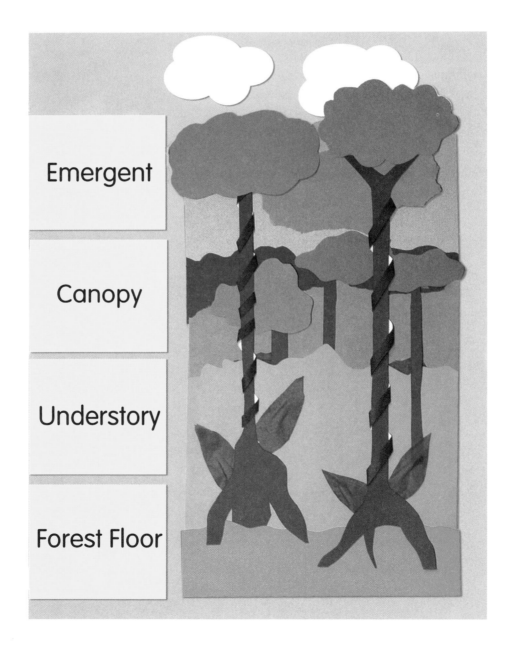

Emergent

Canopy

Understory

Forest Floor

Simple Steps to Show You How

Rainforest Background
- Cover the board in blue butcher paper.
- Create a cut-paper background using several colors of construction paper: orange, light green, bright green, dark green, and gray. Layer the colors and overlap the pieces. Staple them to the blue background.

Trees
- Use different shades of green paper to cut treetops in various sizes.
- Cut trunks for the trees from brown paper. Tuck them into the various layers.
- Wrap a couple of the larger trees in front with brown vines made from thin paper strips.

Labels
- Print a label on yellow paper for each layer of the rainforest.

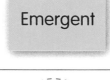

Clouds
- Cut clouds from white paper. Slip them behind the treetops on the blue paper.

Wildlife
- Cut out reproducible pictures of rainforest animals and insects such as the butterfly on page 188 or the snake on page 154. Have children color them, then pin them to the board on the appropriate layer.

Walk in the Rainforest

Children are introduced to plant and animal life found in the Amazon Rainforest. They learn to recognize some common characteristics of a rainforest environment.

Walk in the Rainforest

Walk in the rainforest. What will you see?
Walk in the rainforest. What will there be?

Walk in the rainforest. Look up to see
trees in the rainforest, tall as can be.

2

Walk in the rainforest. Drip, drip, drop, drop.
Rain in the rainforest, when will it stop?

Walk in the rainforest when the rain stops.
Sun on the rainforest, in the treetops.

Walk in the rainforest. Bright flowers grow.
Blooms in the rainforest put on a show.

Walk in the rainforest, green all around.
Plants in the rainforest, shrubs near the ground.

Walk in the rainforest. Who will you meet?
Tribes in the rainforest, people to greet!

Walk in the rainforest, animal sounds!
Life in the rainforest, it's all around.

8

The End

Note: Teachers will make copies and cut in half for minibooks.

Reproducible Story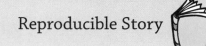

Walk in the Rainforest

Walk in the rainforest.
What will you see?
Walk in the rainforest.
What will there be?

1

Walk in the rainforest.
Look up to see
Trees in the rainforest,
tall as can be.

2

Walk in the rainforest.
Drip, drip, drop, drop.
Rain in the rainforest,
when will it stop?

3

Walk in the rainforest
when the rain stops.
Sun on the rainforest,
in the treetops.

4

Walk in the rainforest.
Bright flowers grow.
Blooms in the rainforest
put on a show.

5

Walk in the rainforest,
green all around.
Plants in the rainforest,
shrubs near the ground.

6

Walk in the rainforest.
Who will you meet?
Tribes in the rainforest,
people to greet!

7

Walk in the rainforest,
animal sounds!
Life in the rainforest,
it's all around.

8

The End

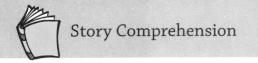
Note: Children color only the pictures of things that live in a rainforest.

Name _____

In the Rainforest

Color the pictures of things that live in a rainforest.

Note: See page 7 for suggestions on using the storyboard pieces on pages 29–33 for Walk in the Rainforest.

Storyboard Pieces

Walk in the Rainforest

©2005 by Evan-Moor Corp.
All About the Rainforest
EMC 2408

Walk in the Rainforest

©2005 by Evan-Moor Corp.
All About the Rainforest
EMC 2408

Walk in the Rainforest

©2005 by Evan-Moor Corp.
All About the Rainforest
EMC 2408

Walk in the Rainforest

©2005 by Evan-Moor Corp.
All About the Rainforest
EMC 2408

Walk in the Rainforest

©2005 by Evan-Moor Corp.
All About the Rainforest
EMC 2408

Walk in the Rainforest

©2005 by Evan-Moor Corp.
All About the Rainforest
EMC 2408

Walk in the Rainforest

©2005 by Evan-Moor Corp.
All About the Rainforest
EMC 2408

Walk in the Rainforest

©2005 by Evan-Moor Corp.
All About the Rainforest
EMC 2408

Walk in the Rainforest

©2005 by Evan-Moor Corp.
All About the Rainforest
EMC 2408

Walk in the Rainforest

©2005 by Evan-Moor Corp.
All About the Rainforest
EMC 2408

Walk in the Rainforest

©2005 by Evan-Moor Corp.
All About the Rainforest • EMC 2408

Rainforest Rain-Shakers

Children create rain rhythms with decorative rain-shakers.

Materials

- page 36, reproduced on green copy paper, one half sheet per child
- toilet paper tube, one per child
- rice and popcorn kernels
- paper plates or bowls
- scissors
- glue
- stapler

Preparation

1. Once page 36 has been reproduced, cut the pages in half. Give each child one half.
2. Place the rice and popcorn kernels on separate plates or in separate bowls.

Steps to Follow

1. Children take a toilet paper tube and the rainforest pattern. They turn the pattern over and spread glue around the edges and in the center. Children wrap the pattern around the tube.
2. The teacher staples one side of each child's tube closed.
3. Children count out 20 popcorn kernels and drop them into the tube.
4. The children then take ten "pinches" of rice and drop them into the tube.
5. The teacher staples the remaining open side of each child's tube closed.
6. Children use the rain-shakers to accompany the song "Rain-Shaker Rhythms" on page 37.

Note: Reproduce this pattern to use with Rainforest Rain-Shakers art activity.

All About the Rainforest • EMC 2408 • ©2005 by Evan-Moor Corp.

Note: Use the Rainforest Rain-Shakers
on page 35 to accompany this chant.

Art Activity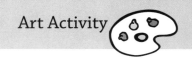

Rain-Shaker Rhythms

Rain-shaker rhythms
(Shake shake shake)
Rhythms help us count
1, 2, 3!

Rain-shaker rhythms
(Shake shake shake)
Rhythms help us count
4, 5, 6!

Rain-shaker rhythms
(Shake shake shake)
Rhythms help us count
7, 8, 9!

(Continue chant to 20.)

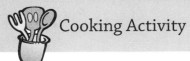

Cooking Activity

Note: Check for allergies before beginning any cooking activity.
An allergic reaction can occur through taste, smell, or contact with allergens.

This tropical snack is made with products originally found in rainforests: bananas, orange juice, and chocolate, which is made from cacao beans.

Rainforest Treats

Preparation

1. Prepare a cooking center with all materials assembled.
2. Slice the bananas.
3. Fill small paper cups with orange juice, one cup per child.
4. Place chocolate sprinkles on several paper plates.

Steps to Follow

1. Children pierce a banana slice with a toothpick.
2. They dip the banana slice into their cup of orange juice and then lay it on the chocolate sprinkles, covering all sides. Then they place it on a paper plate.
3. Children enjoy their Rainforest Treat!

Extension

Provide other foods from the rainforest for children to sample such as papaya, avocado, passion fruit, pineapple, cashews, Brazil nuts, and shredded dried coconut.

Materials

- 2 to 3 banana slices per child
- orange juice
- chocolate sprinkles
- toothpicks
- paper plates
- small paper cups
- knife
- cutting board

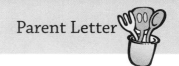

Dear Parent(s) or Guardian(s),

Today we cooked in class. Your child helped prepare "Rainforest Treats." The ingredients were all originally found in the rainforest. Besides having fun cooking and eating, the children practiced these skills:

- listening to and following directions
- vocabulary development
- using small motor skills

For our unit *The Rainforest*, we will send home a variety of new recipes. Each recipe will be one that your child has tried in class and is excited about. We hope you have an opportunity to try this recipe again with your child. Allowing your child to help you in the kitchen is a wonderful way to reinforce learning skills while creating family memories.

Rainforest Treats

Materials

- 2 to 3 banana slices per person
- orange juice, 1 small cupful per person
- chocolate sprinkles
- toothpicks
- small plate

Steps to Follow

1. Slice bananas. Fill a cup with orange juice. Place chocolate sprinkles on a plate.
2. Pierce a banana slice with a toothpick.
3. Dip the banana slice into the cup of orange juice and then lay it on the chocolate sprinkles. Cover all sides. Place it on a plate.
4. Enjoy your Rainforest Treats!

Walking in the Rainforest

Draw a picture of yourself. Write your name.

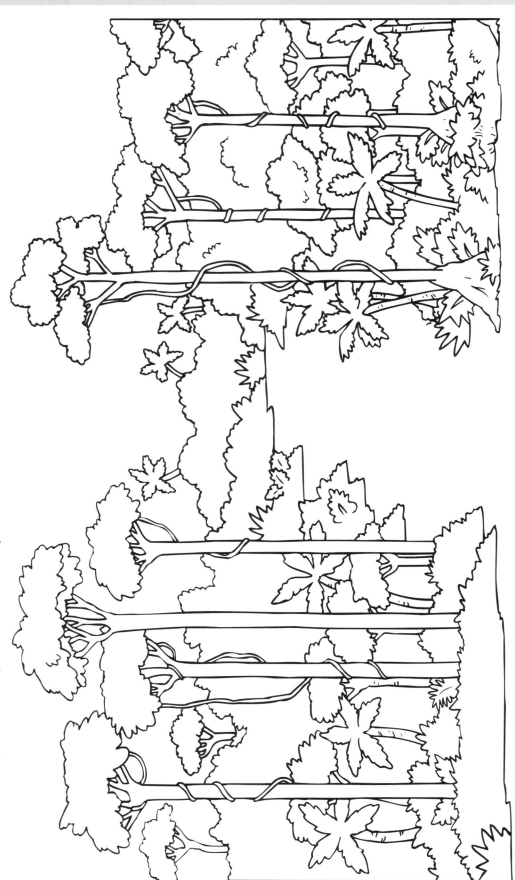

_____ is in the rainforest.

Note: Children mark the path from 1 to 20 in sequential order.

Math—Number Order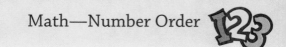

Name _____

Rainforest Campsite

Mark a path to the tent.

Follow the numbers in order.

Note: Children cut out and glue the pictures to complete the patterns.

Name _____

What's Missing?

Cut ✂ the pictures. Glue 🖊 them to complete the patterns.

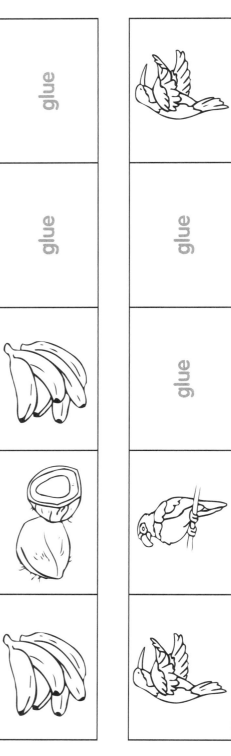
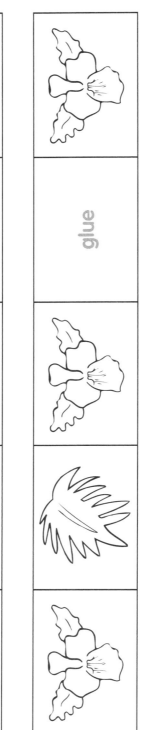

Raindrops

Working independently or in pairs, children place the correct number of raindrops on each leaf.

Materials

- pages 44 and 45, reproduced
- page 46, reproduced, one per child
- green copy paper or construction paper
- blue or white copy paper or construction paper
- marking pen
- scissors
- sturdy envelope or folder

Creating the Center

1. Reproduce 11 copies of page 44 on green copy paper, or use the leaf as a template to trace onto green construction paper. Number the leaves from 0 through 10. Laminate and cut out the leaves.

2. Reproduce 5 copies of page 45 on white or blue paper. Laminate the copies, then cut apart.

3. Store the center pieces in a sturdy envelope or folder.

4. Reproduce page 46 and keep a supply at the center.

5. Plan time to model how the center is used.

Using the Center

1. Children lay out all the leaves on a flat surface.

2. Then they count out the correct number of raindrops and place them on each leaf.

3. Once children complete the center activity, they complete One Big Leaf math activity on page 46.

Note: Reproduce this pattern to use with Raindrops center activity.

Leaf

Note: Reproduce this pattern to use with Raindrops center activity.

Center Activity Pattern Pieces

Raindrops

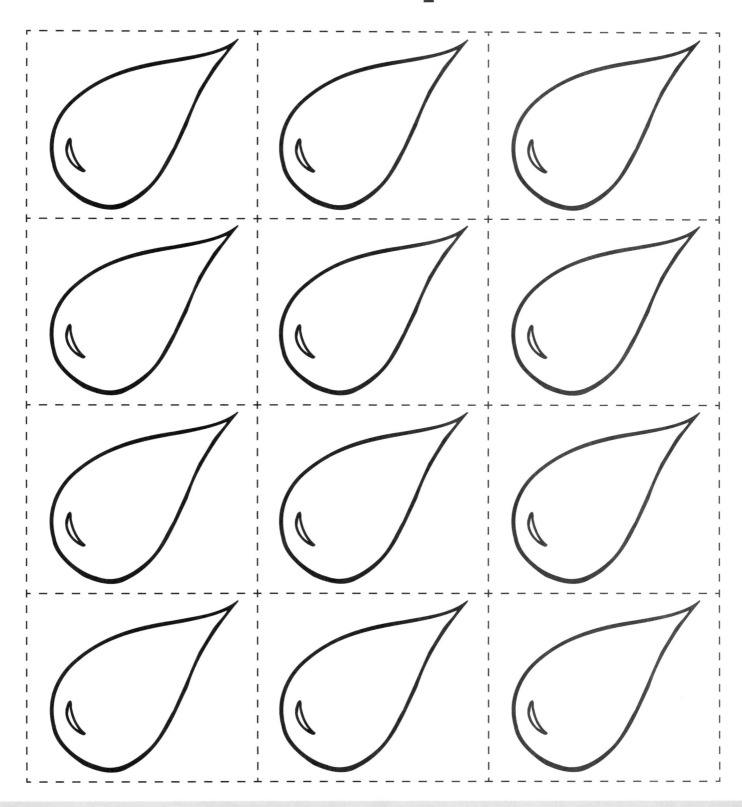

 **Center Activity**

Name _____

One Big Leaf

Connect the dots.

Then draw 10 raindrops on the leaf .

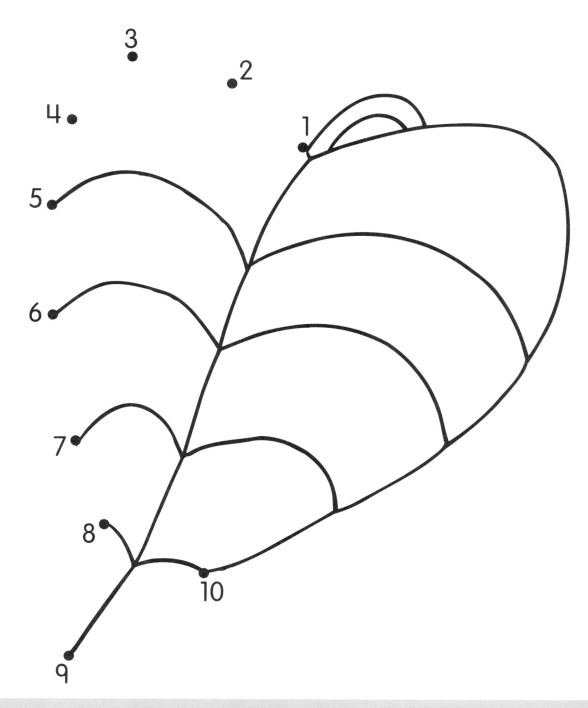

All About the Rainforest • EMC 2408 • ©2005 by Evan-Moor Corp.

Children create lively weather sound effects for the story "Weather Ride."

Weather Ride

Preparation

1. Familiarize yourself with the story "Weather Ride" on page 48.

2. Explain to children that they are going to make "weather sounds" while you read the story.

3. Divide the class into four groups. Each group will make a different sound effect:

   - **light rain** (slowly snapping fingers or clicking tongues),
   - **heavy rain** (rubbing hands quickly together),
   - **wind** (whistling or blowing), and
   - **thunderstorm** (stomping feet).

4. Have each group practice making their assigned weather sound. Once groups have practiced, read the story and ask children to accompany it with their weather sounds.

Weather Ride

We began our ride early one hot summer morning deep in the jungles of South America. As we rumbled through the jungle in our old jeep, the squealing monkeys swung from branch to branch overhead. Brightly colored birds squawked and swooped close to our heads. Ferocious jaguars roared loudly as they sunned themselves on large rocks in the clearing. The sun shined brightly until a ***light rain*** began to fall in the jungle (pause, then cue to stop).

After a short while, the rain turned into a ***heavy rain*** (pause). The animals in the jungle began to scatter (cue to stop) as the ***wind*** blew through the coconut trees (pause). Suddenly, (cue to stop) a crack of thunder signaled the start of an unexpected ***thunderstorm*** (pause). We had to stop our jeep because the blinding rain kept us from seeing the path we were following.

The ***thunderstorm*** (continues) lasted only a short time (cue to stop) until it calmed to a ***heavy rain*** (pause, then cue to stop). The ***wind*** whistled again (pause), and then it suddenly stopped (cue to stop). The ***heavy rain*** (pause, then cue to stop) slowed to a ***light rain*** once again (pause, then cue to stop). The monkeys began their chatter once more, and the jaguars returned to their place in the sun. We started the old jeep and continued deeper into the jungle.

Note: Sing this song to the tune of "Twinkle, Twinkle Little Star."

Music/Dramatic Play Activity

Rainforest Song

Children create movements to accompany this familiar tune.

Listen, listen, walk with me.
Can you hear it? What can it be?
Take a rain walk, come with me.
Through the forest and the trees.
Listen, listen, walk with me.
Can you hear it? What can it be?

Listen, listen, to the beat.
Walk the rain beat with your feet.
Walk the rain beat on the one.
One-two-one-two-one-two-one.
Listen, listen, to the beat.
Walk the rain beat with your feet.

Listen, listen, have some fun.
Jump up high to bring the sun.
Jump up high when I count one.
One-two-one-two-one-two-one.

Listen, listen, have some fun.
Jump up high to bring the sun.

Now our rain walk has to end,
Someday soon we'll walk again.

Up into the Rainforest

Children are introduced to the four levels of the rainforest:
forest floor, understory, canopy, and emergent layer.

Up into the Rainforest

A little ant looked out from the
shady forest floor and said,

"I am king of the rainforest."

A sleepy bat looked out from the understory of small trees and said,

"I am king of the rainforest."

A spider monkey looked out from the green umbrella canopy of tall treetops and said,

"I am king of the rainforest!"

A harpy eagle looked down from the emergent layer of high trees and said,

"I don't think so!"

The End

Note: Teachers will make copies and cut in half for minibooks.

Reproducible Story

Up into the Rainforest

A little ant looked out from the shady forest floor and said,

1

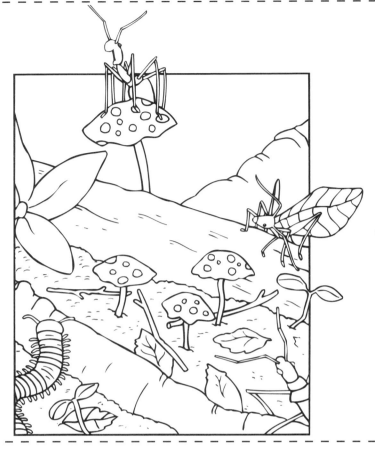

"I am king of
the rainforest."

2

A sleepy bat
looked out from the
understory of small
trees and said,

3

"I am king of
the rainforest."

4

A spider monkey
looked out from
the green umbrella
canopy of tall
treetops and said,

5

"I am king of
the rainforest!"

6

A harpy eagle looked
down from the
emergent layer of
high trees and said,

7

"I don't think so!"

8

The End

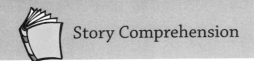

Note: Children draw a line from each animal to the correct rainforest layer as presented in the Up into the Rainforest story.

Name _____

Where in the Rainforest?

Color. Match.

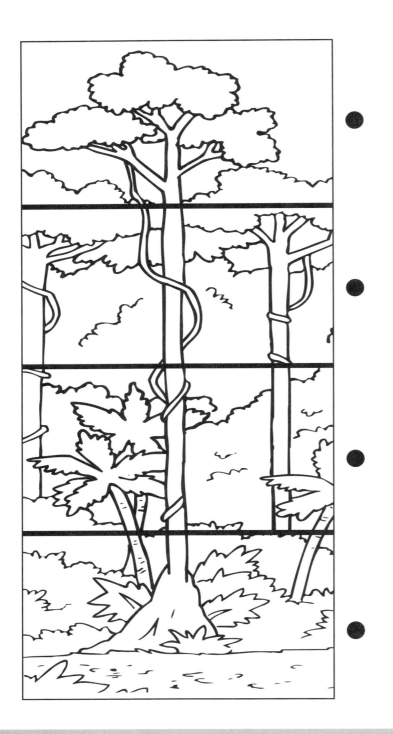

Note: See page 7 for suggestions on using the storyboard pieces on pages 67 and 69 for Up into the Rainforest.

Storyboard Pieces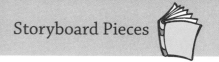

Forest floor

Understory

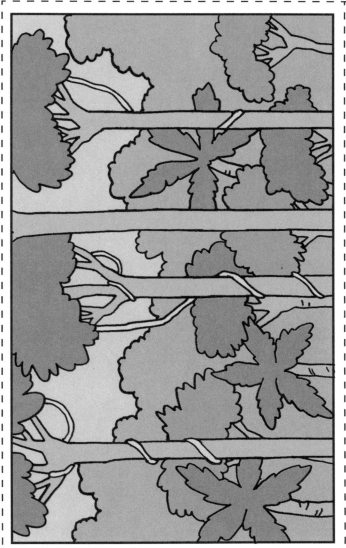

Emergent

Up into the Rainforest

Canopy

Up into the Rainforest

Up into
the Rainforest

Up into
the Rainforest

Rainforest Layers

Children make a mobile showing the four layers of the rainforest.

Materials

- pages 72 and 73, reproduced, one per child
- construction paper cut into rectangles, six per child
- yarn
- scissors
- crayons
- glue
- hole punch

Preparation

1. Cut 4 rectangles of construction paper on which children glue the rainforest layers.

2. Cut 2 rectangles of construction paper on which children glue the labels.

3. Explain to children that they are going to make a rainforest mobile that will include the four layers of the rainforest. Review the layers of the rainforest: forest floor, small plants and trees (understory), tall trees that form an "umbrella" (canopy), and the highest trees (emergent).

Steps to Follow

1. Children color and cut out the rainforest pictures and labels.

2. Then they glue the pictures and labels onto the appropriate pieces of construction paper.

3. Children punch holes in the pieces where indicated. (Younger children may need assistance.)

4. Then children put the rainforest layers in order. An adult assists the children in tying the layers together with yarn to form a mobile.

Art Activity Pattern Pieces

Note: Reproduce these patterns to use with Rainforest Layers art activity.

Rainforest

Emergent

Canopy

Note: Reproduce these patterns to use with Rainforest Layers art activity.

Art Activity Pattern Pieces

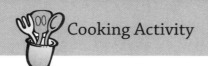 **Cooking Activity**

Note: Check for allergies before beginning any cooking activity.
An allergic reaction can occur through taste, smell, or contact with allergens.

Use this fun dessert to teach children about the delicate balance of nature on the rainforest floor.

Worms and Dirt

Preparation

1. Prepare the instant pudding mix as directed on the package.

2. Explain to children that the soil in the rainforest is very old. Dead leaves, logs, and other things help the soil become "new" again. Ants and worms also help make the soil new again by breaking it down. This makes food for the trees.

3. Plan time to model the steps for this project and a completed Worms and Dirt cup.

Steps to Follow

1. Children place vanilla wafers in a plastic self-locking bag and crush them with the rolling pin.

2. Then children spoon ¼ cup chocolate pudding, or "dirt," into a plastic cup.

3. They push two gummy worms into the dirt.

4. Children sprinkle the dirt with the wafer crumbs, or "leaf litter."

5. Children enjoy their Worms and Dirt snack!

Extension

Have children collect leaves. Place them on a windowsill and observe what happens to them over a week's time.

Materials

- 16 oz. (448 g) box instant chocolate pudding mix (one box = eight ¼-cup servings)

- milk

- vanilla wafers, four per child

- gummy worms, two per child

- large mixing bowl

- large spoon

- small plastic self-locking bags, one per child

- rolling pin

- whisk

- clear plastic cups

- plastic spoons

Dear Parent(s) or Guardian(s),

Today we cooked in class. Your child prepared "Worms and Dirt." Your child learned that the soil in the rainforest is very old. Dead leaves, logs, and other things help the soil become "new" again. Ants and worms also help make the soil new again by breaking it down. This makes food for the trees. Besides having fun cooking and eating, the children practiced these skills:

- vocabulary development
- listening to and following directions
- using small motor skills

For our unit *The Rainforest*, we will send home a variety of new recipes. Each recipe will be one that your child has tried in class and is excited about. We hope you have an opportunity to try this recipe again with your child. Allowing your child to help you in the kitchen is a wonderful way to reinforce learning skills while creating family memories.

Worms and Dirt

Materials

- 16 oz. (448 g) box instant chocolate pudding mix (one box = eight ¼-cup servings)
- 2 cups milk
- vanilla wafers, 3 or 4 per person
- gummy worms
- large mixing bowl
- large spoon
- plastic self-locking bag
- rolling pin
- whisk
- clear plastic cups
- plastic spoons

Steps to Follow

1. Prepare the instant pudding mix as directed on the package.
2. Place vanilla wafers in a plastic self-locking bag and crush them with the rolling pin.
3. Spoon ¼ cup chocolate pudding, or "dirt," into a plastic cup.
4. Push two gummy worms into the dirt.
5. Sprinkle the dirt with the vanilla wafer crumbs, or "leaf litter."
6. Enjoy your Worms and Dirt snack!

Name _____

Where Are They?

Listen, then color.

Note: Children count the objects below and write the correct number in the box beside • each picture.

Math—Counting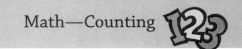

Name _____

In the Canopy

Count and write.

What Lives Here?

Creating the Center

1. Laminate and cut apart pages 79 through 85.

2. Place the rainforest layer task cards in one envelope and the animal and plant task cards in another envelope.

3. Place both envelopes in a sturdy folder or large envelope.

4. Plan time to model how the center is used.

Using the Center

1. Children may use the center individually or with a partner.

2. Children lay out the rainforest layer task cards in order from forest floor to emergent.

3. Then they place the correct plant and animal task cards on or beside each rainforest layer.

4. Children self-check their answers by matching the color border on each card to the color border on each rainforest layer.

Children match rainforest plants and animals with the appropriate layers of the rainforest.

Materials

- pages 79–85, laminated

- envelopes

- scissors

- sturdy folder or large envelope

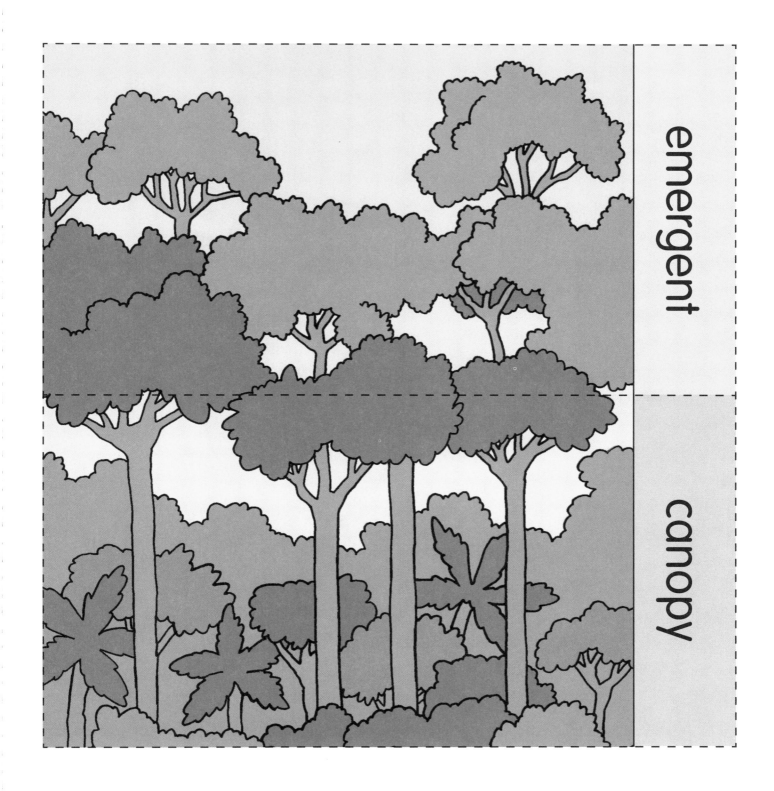

emergent

canopy

What Lives Here?

©2005 by Evan-Moor Corp.
All About the Rainforest • EMC 2408

What Lives Here?

©2005 by Evan-Moor Corp.
All About the Rainforest • EMC 2408

understory

forest floor

What Lives Here?

©2005 by Evan-Moor Corp.
All About the Rainforest • EMC 2408

What Lives Here?

©2005 by Evan-Moor Corp.
All About the Rainforest • EMC 2408

harpy eagle

hummingbird

flower

tree frog

sloth

monkey

flower

toucan

snake

What Lives Here?

What Lives Here?

What Lives Here?

What Lives Here?

What Lives Here?

What Lives Here?

What Lives Here?

What Lives Here?

What Lives Here?

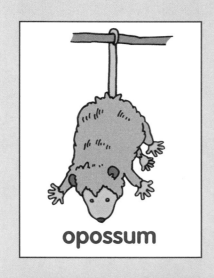

opossum

bat

butterfly

tree

anaconda

tapir

alligator

ant

jaguar

What Lives Here?

What Lives Here?

What Lives Here?

What Lives Here?

What Lives Here?

What Lives Here?

What Lives Here?

What Lives Here?

What Lives Here?

Children play a game with partners and follow the leader's commands.

Sleepy Bat

Preparation

1. Plan to play in a large outdoor space.

2. Explain to children that a fruit bat is one of the animals in the understory of the rainforest. Tell them that bats sleep all day and come out at night. Then tell children that they will be the "bats" in this game.

How to Play

1. The teacher is the leader.

2. Each bat chooses a partner.

3. The leader calls out instructions: *Stand back to back. Face each other and stand knee to knee. Now stand straight up. Hold hands,* etc.

4. The leader calls out, *Go to sleep now, bats!* All the bats squat down and pretend to be sleeping.

5. When the leader calls out, *Wake up, sleepy bats!* all the bats must find a new partner. Once every bat has a partner, begin giving instructions again.

Note: Sing this song to the tune of "The Mulberry Bush."

Here We Go Round the Rainforest Tree

(Hold hands and move in a circle.)
Here we go round the rainforest tree,
The rainforest tree, the rainforest tree.
Here we go round the rainforest tree.
We're on the **forest floor**.
(Drop to sitting position.)

(Hold hands and move in a circle.)
Here we go to the **understory**,
The understory, the understory.
Here we go to the understory.
We're climbing up some more.
(Climb a ladder.)

(Hold hands and move in a circle.)
Here we go into the **canopy**,
The canopy, the canopy.
Here we go into the canopy.
We're climbing up some more.
(Climb a ladder.)

(Hold hands and move in a circle.)
Now we are in the **emergent** trees,
Emergent trees, emergent trees.
Now we are in the emergent trees,
And we can climb no more.
(Drop to sitting position.)

Extension

Children wear their Rainforest Explorer visors while singing this song.

Children sing a song while pretending they are climbing up through the various layers of the rainforest.

Note: Reproduce this pattern for each child to color and cut out. An adult pulls a string through the holes. Children wear the visor while singing "Here We Go Round the Rainforest Tree."

Music/Dramatic Play Activity Pattern Piece

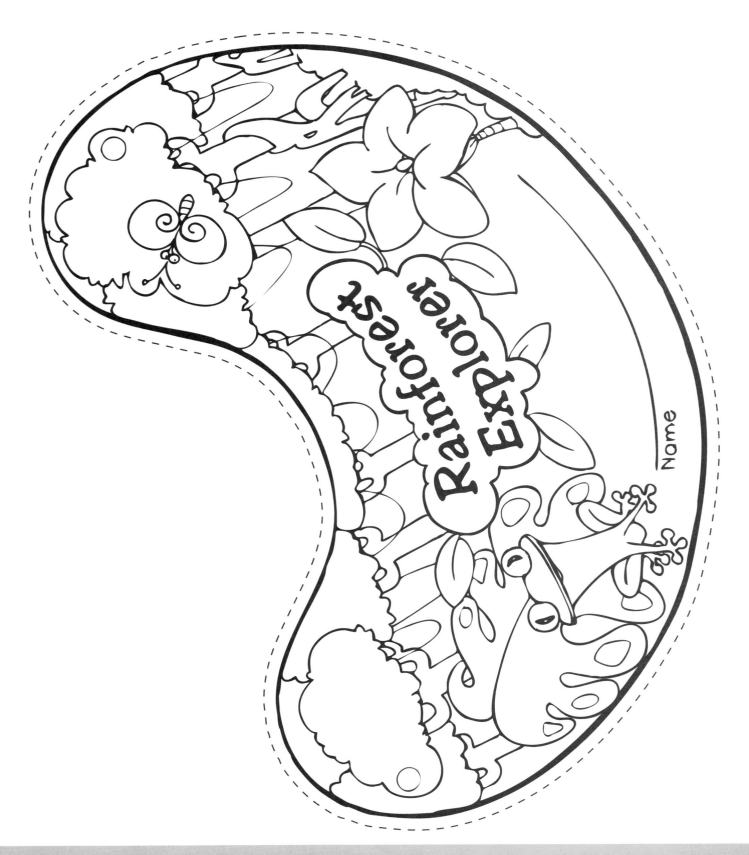

3

Rainforest Plants

Children are introduced to some of
the plants that grow in the Amazon Rainforest.

Plants, Plants, Plants

So many plants, rainforest plants.
Trees are the tallest of all.

So many plants, rainforest plants.
Roots above-ground hold them tall.

So many plants, rainforest plants.
Some flowers open at night.

So many plants, rainforest plants.
These flowers give bees delight.

So many plants, rainforest plants.
Some grow on branches of trees.

So many plants, rainforest plants.
Some can trap bugs in their leaves.

So many plants, rainforest plants.
Growing in so many ways.

So many plants, rainforest plants.
Growing since dinosaur days.

99

The End

Note: Teachers will make copies and cut in half for minibooks.

Reproducible Story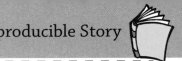

Plants, Plants, Plants

So many plants,
rainforest plants.
Trees are the
tallest of all.

1

So many plants,
rainforest plants.
Roots above-ground
hold them tall.

2

So many plants,
rainforest plants.
Some flowers open
at night.

3

So many plants,
rainforest plants.
These flowers give
bees delight.

4

So many plants,
rainforest plants.
Some grow on
branches of trees.

5

So many plants,
rainforest plants.
Some can trap
bugs in their
leaves.

6

So many plants,
rainforest plants.
Growing in so
many ways.

7

So many plants,
rainforest plants.
Growing since
dinosaur days.

8

The End

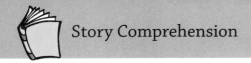

Story Comprehension

Note: Children color the pictures from the story Plants, Plants, Plants.

Name _____

Does It Grow
in the Rainforest?

Color the pictures that show things that grow in the rainforest.

Note: See page 8 for suggestions on using the storyboard pieces on pages 107 and 109 for Plants, Plants, Plants.

Storyboard Pieces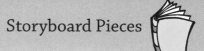

Rainforest Plants

©2005 by Evan-Moor Corp.
All About the Rainforest • EMC 2408

Rainforest Plants

©2005 by Evan-Moor Corp.
All About the Rainforest • EMC 2408

Rainforest Plants

©2005 by Evan-Moor Corp.
All About the Rainforest • EMC 2408

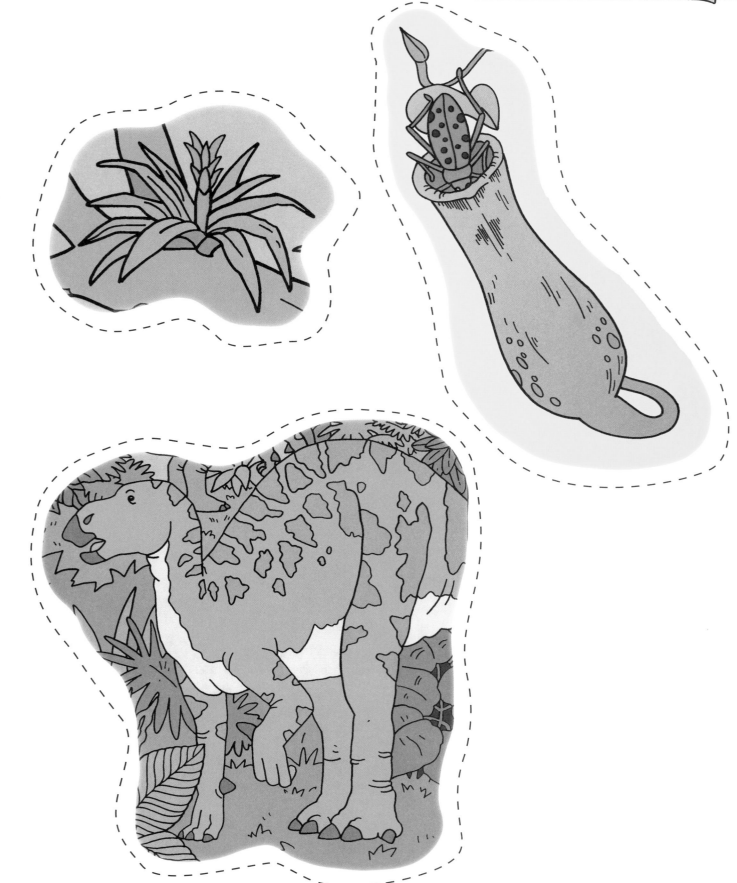

Rainforest Plants   **109**

Rainforest Plants

Rainforest Plants

Rainforest Plants

Children create a leaf-rubbing home for rainforest insects and flowers.

Materials

- page 112, reproduced several times
- 9" × 12" (23 × 30.5 cm) white drawing paper, one sheet per child
- various large leaves
- crayons (remove wrappers)
- glue
- scissors

Rainforest Rubbings

Preparation

1. Collect green fern fronds or other leaves from outdoors, or ask a florist for clippings of greens that would otherwise be tossed. Try experimenting to see which leaves make the best prints.

2. Plan time to model how to make a leaf rubbing. Model a completed Rainforest Rubbings art project.

Steps to Follow

1. Children choose several leaves and place them facedown on the table.

2. They place a sheet of white drawing paper on top of the leaves.

3. Then children hold the paper and leaves in place and use the side of an unwrapped crayon to rub firmly over the leaves.

4. Children choose pictures from page 112 to color, cut out, and glue onto their leaf rubbings.

Extension

Make a mural using white bulletin board paper and the leaf-rubbing technique. Have children paint flowers, insects, and animals on it.

Note: Reproduce these patterns to use with Rainforest Rubbings art activity.

Note: Check for allergies before beginning any cooking activity.
An allergic reaction can occur through taste, smell, or contact with allergens.

Cooking Activity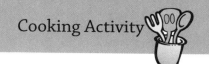

Children prepare a fruity snack made from ingredients indigenous to tropical rainforests.

Materials

Makes 20 servings

- 2½ cups (385 g) dried mixed papaya, mango, and pineapple bits

- 1½ cups (120 g) banana chips

- ¾ cup (60 g) shredded baking coconut

- ¾ cup (110 g) chocolate chips

- medium mixing bowl

- large spoon

- measuring cups

- plastic snack-sized self-locking bags, one per child

Rainforest Trail Mix

Preparation

1. Prepare a cooking center with all materials assembled.

2. Plan time to review measurement. (You may wish to mark the measuring cups so that younger children can easily complete the measurements.)

3. Plan time to model the steps.

4. Explain to children that many kinds of fruits grow in the rainforest. Tell children that the fruits provide food for the animals.

Steps to Follow

1. Children take turns measuring the various ingredients and pouring them into a mixing bowl.

2. They take turns stirring the mixture with a spoon.

3. Each child scoops a small serving of trail mix into a measuring cup and then pours it into a snack-size plastic bag.

4. Children enjoy eating their Rainforest Trail Mix!

Parent Letter

Dear Parent(s) or Guardian(s),

Today we cooked in class. Your child helped prepare "Rainforest Trail Mix." The class learned that many fruits grow in the rainforest, providing food for the animals. The ingredients in our snack are indigenous to tropical rainforests. Besides having fun cooking and eating, the children practiced these skills:

- vocabulary development
- listening to and following directions
- using small motor skills
- measurement

For our unit *The Rainforest*, we will send home a variety of new recipes. Each recipe will be one that your child has tried in class and is excited about. We hope you have an opportunity to try this recipe again with your child. Allowing your child to help you in the kitchen is a wonderful way to reinforce learning skills while creating family memories.

Rainforest Trail Mix

Materials

Makes 20 servings

- 2½ cups (385 g) dried mixed papaya, mango, and pineapple bits
- 1½ cups (120 g) banana chips
- ¾ cup (60 g) shredded baking coconut
- ¾ cup (110 g) chocolate chips
- medium mixing bowl
- spoon
- measuring cup
- plastic snack-sized self-locking bags

Steps to Follow

1. Help your child measure and then pour all ingredients into a mixing bowl.
2. Stir the mixture with a spoon.
3. Scoop small servings of trail mix into plastic snack-sized self-locking bags.
4. Enjoy your Rainforest Trail Mix!

Note: Review color words with children. You may wish to display a chart with the colors and their names as a guide for young learners.

Language—Identifying Color Words ABC

Name _____

Rainforest Flowers

Trace and color.

red

blue

yellow

green

Name _____

Rainforest Food

Color the pictures in each row that are the same.

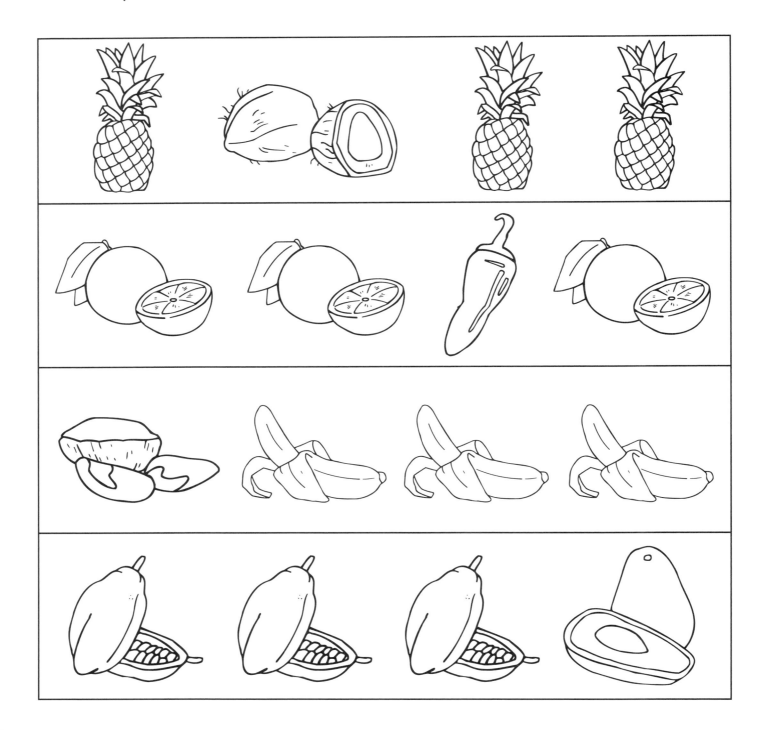

Note: Children count the seeds and write the number in the box.

Math—Counting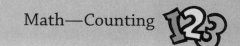

Name _____

How Many Seeds?

Count and write.

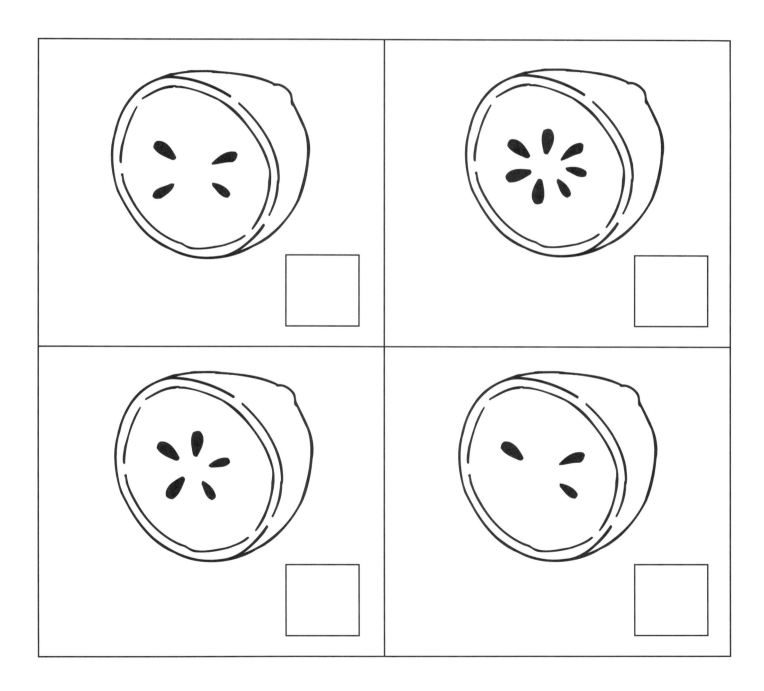

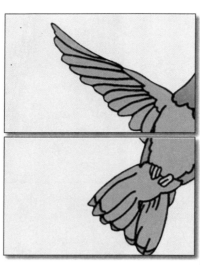

Working independently or in pairs, children put together rainforest puzzles.

Rainforest Puzzles

Creating the Center

1. Laminate and cut apart pages 119 and 121.

2. Place each puzzle in its own envelope. Label the envelopes.

3. Place the puzzle envelopes in a sturdy folder or box with a lid.

4. Plan time to model how the center is used.

Using the Center

1. Children may use the center individually or with a partner.

2. Children put together one or more of the puzzles.

Materials

- pages 119 and 121, laminated

- scissors

- four envelopes

- sturdy folder or box with a lid

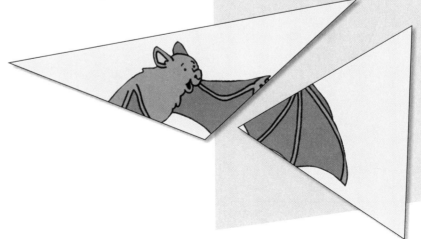

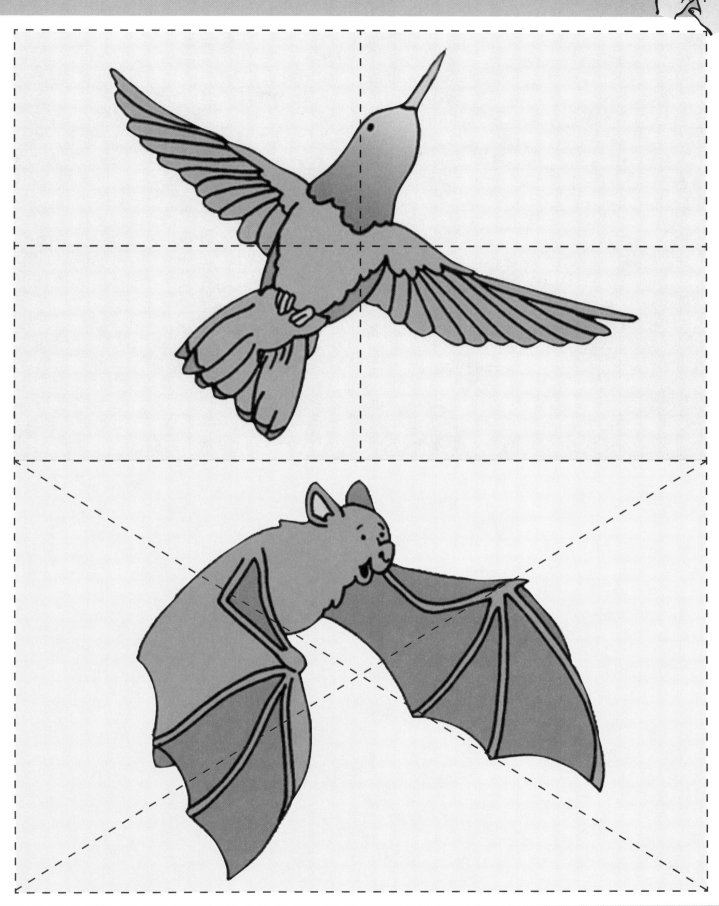

Rainforest Puzzles

©2005 by Evan-Moor Corp.
All About the Rainforest • EMC 2408

Rainforest Puzzles

©2005 by Evan-Moor Corp.
All About the Rainforest • EMC 2408

Rainforest Puzzles

©2005 by Evan-Moor Corp.
All About the Rainforest • EMC 2408

Rainforest Puzzles

©2005 by Evan-Moor Corp.
All About the Rainforest • EMC 2408

Rainforest Puzzles

©2005 by Evan-Moor Corp.
All About the Rainforest • EMC 2408

Rainforest Puzzles

©2005 by Evan-Moor Corp.
All About the Rainforest • EMC 2408

Rainforest Puzzles

©2005 by Evan-Moor Corp.
All About the Rainforest • EMC 2408

Rainforest Puzzles

©2005 by Evan-Moor Corp.
All About the Rainforest • EMC 2408

Rainforest Puzzles

©2005 by Evan-Moor Corp.
All About the Rainforest • EMC 2408

Rainforest Puzzles

©2005 by Evan-Moor Corp.
All About the Rainforest • EMC 2408

Rainforest Puzzles

©2005 by Evan-Moor Corp.
All About the Rainforest • EMC 2408

Rainforest Puzzles

©2005 by Evan-Moor Corp.
All About the Rainforest • EMC 2408

Rainforest Puzzles

©2005 by Evan-Moor Corp.
All About the Rainforest • EMC 2408

Rainforest Puzzles

©2005 by Evan-Moor Corp.
All About the Rainforest • EMC 2408

Rainforest Puzzles

©2005 by Evan-Moor Corp.
All About the Rainforest • EMC 2408

Rainforest Puzzles

©2005 by Evan-Moor Corp.
All About the Rainforest • EMC 2408

Children become rainforest trees dancing in the wind when they wear these leafy headbands.

Materials

- page 124, reproduced, one per child
- 12" x 18" (30.5 x 45.5 cm) sheets of brown construction paper
- green crepe-paper streamers, four per child
- glue
- tape
- scissors
- crayons

Dancing Trees

Preparation

1. Cut brown construction paper lengthwise into strips for headbands. Each child will need two strips to make a headband.
2. Cut four 12" (30.5 cm) strips of green crepe paper for each child.

Steps to Follow

1. Children take two strips of brown paper to an adult to assemble a headband. Tape the pieces together.
2. Then children color, cut out, and glue the leaves and rhyme to their headband.
3. Children twist four strips of green crepe paper and glue them between the leaves on their headband.
4. Once the glue dries, children go outside and begin their outdoor activity.

How to Play

Children wear their tree headbands and do the following:

- grow from a small tree into a tall tree
- stand still and be a tall tree
- run and be a tree with blowing leaves
- be a small tree in the understory layer
- be a very tall tree in the emergent layer
- act like a tree dancing in the wind

Note: Reproduce these patterns to use with Dancing Trees outdoor activity.

Rainforest trees blow in the breeze.

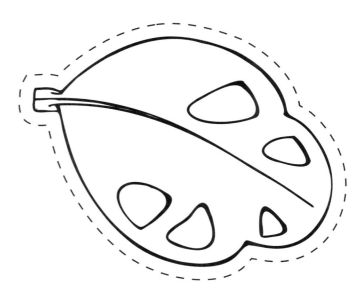

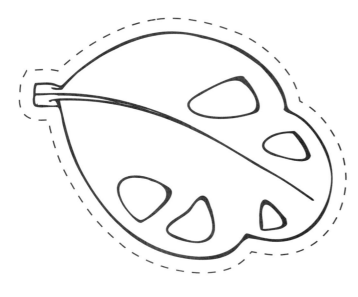

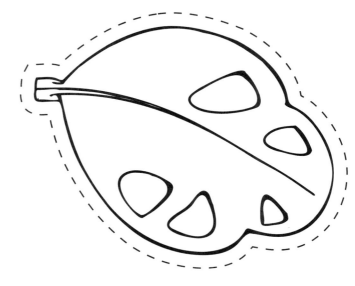

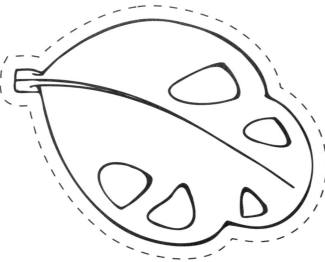

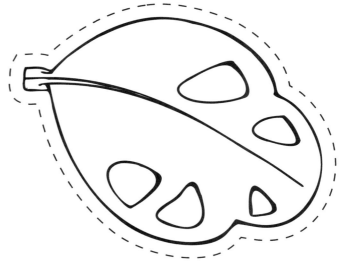

Note: Sing this song to the tune of "The Farmer in the Dell."

Music/Dramatic Play Activity

In this musical skit, children sing about the plants and animals of the rainforest. Divide the children into "plants" and "animals" for this skit.

Trees, Leaves, and Logs

These trees are homes for birds.
These trees are homes for birds.
Trees in the rainforest are homes
for birds.

("Plants" stand with arms up like trees.
"Animals" fly between the trees.)

These leaves are homes for frogs.
These leaves are homes for frogs.
Leaves in the rainforest are homes
for frogs.

(Plants stand in a circle.
Animals hop in and out of the circle.)

These logs are homes for ants.
These logs are homes for ants.
Logs in the rainforest are homes
for ants.

(Plants lie on the ground like logs.
Animals crawl between them.)

Extension

Invite children to make up some more verses to sing about other animals that live in and around the rainforest plants.

Rainforest Animals

Children learn about some of the animals
that live in rainforests.

Rainforest Animals

Come out, hummingbird.
Zip around and fly in place.
Come out, little hummingbird.

1

Come out, piranha.
Show your sharp teeth.
Come out, hungry piranha.

2

Come out, frog.
Climb with your sticky toe pads.
Come out, tree frog.

3

Come out, capybara.
Swim for your dinner.
Come out, fat capybara.

4

Come out, butterfly.
Flutter in the dim forest.
Come out, pretty butterfly.

Come out, toucan.
Look for fruit and bugs.
Come out, busy toucan.

Come out, anaconda.
Open wide to eat your catch.
Come out, big anaconda.

Come out, jaguar.
Climb a tree and keep watch.
Come out, fast jaguar.

The End

Note: Teachers will make copies
and cut in half for minibooks.

Reproducible Story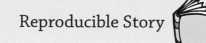

Rainforest Animals

Come out,
hummingbird.
Zip around and
fly in place.
Come out, little
hummingbird.

1

Come out, piranha.

Show your sharp teeth.

Come out, hungry piranha.

2

Come out, frog.

Climb with your

sticky toe pads.

Come out, tree frog.

3

Come out, capybara.

Swim for your dinner.

Come out, fat capybara.

4

Come out, butterfly.

Flutter in the dim forest.

Come out, pretty butterfly.

5

Come out, toucan.

Look for fruit and bugs.

Come out, busy toucan.

6

Come out,
anaconda.
Open wide to
eat your catch.
Come out,
big anaconda.

7

Come out, jaguar.
Climb a tree and
keep watch.
Come out, fast jaguar.

8

The End

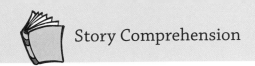

Name _____

It's Fun to Match!

Match. Draw a line.

Toucans eat

water

Piranha live in the

tree
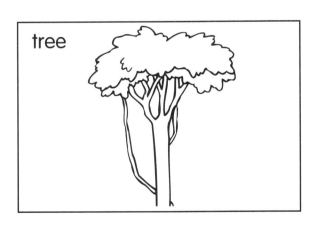

Tree frogs live in a
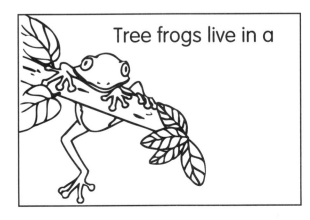

berries

Note: See page 8 for suggestions on using the storyboard pieces on pages 143–147 for Rainforest Animals.

Storyboard Pieces
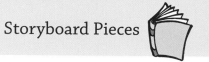

Rainforest Animals

Rainforest Animals

Rainforest Animals

Rainforest Animals

Rainforest Animals

©2005 by Evan-Moor Corp.
All About the Rainforest • EMC 2408

Rainforest Animals

©2005 by Evan-Moor Corp.
All About the Rainforest • EMC 2408

Rainforest Animals

©2005 by Evan-Moor Corp.
All About the Rainforest • EMC 2408

Rainforest Animals

©2005 by Evan-Moor Corp.
All About the Rainforest • EMC 2408

Rainforest
Animals

©2005 by Evan-Moor Corp.
All About the Rainforest
EMC 2408

Rainforest Animals

©2005 by Evan-Moor Corp.
All About the Rainforest • EMC 2408

Rainforest Animals

©2005 by Evan-Moor Corp.
All About the Rainforest • EMC 2408

Hummingbird Hideaway

Steps to Follow

Children make a hummingbird stick puppet that hides behind a flower.

Materials

- craft stick, one per child
- page 150, reproduced, one per child
- paper fastener, one per child
- scissors
- glue
- crayons

1. Children color and cut out the hummingbird and flower on page 150.

2. Then they glue the back of the flower to a craft stick.

3. Children attach the hummingbird behind the flower by poking a paper fastener through the flower and the bird at the dot (adult assistance required). This will allow the bird to swivel and hide behind the flower.

4. Children recite the chant below while making their hummingbird disappear behind the flower.

Little Hummingbird

Little hummingbird,

A flower it sees.

Little hummingbird,

Quick as a breeze.

Little hummingbird,

Takes a sip.

Little hummingbird,

Goes away, zip!

Art Activity Pattern Pieces

Note: Reproduce these patterns to use with Hummingbird Hideaway art activity.

Note: Check for allergies before beginning any cooking activity.
An allergic reaction can occur through taste, smell, or contact with allergens.

Cooking Activity

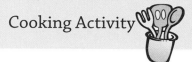

Children prepare butterfly treats using mandarin oranges for wings and shredded cheese for antennae.

Materials

- graham cracker squares, one per child
- cream cheese spread
- green food coloring
- mandarin orange slices, two per child
- shredded cheese, two shreds per child
- dull plastic knife
- spoon
- paper plate, one per child
- small mixing bowl
- can opener

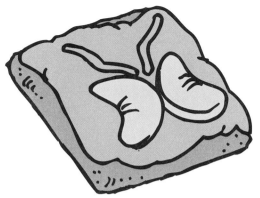

Butterfly Treats

Preparation

1. Prepare a cooking center with all materials assembled.
2. Color the cream cheese with a few drops of green food coloring and mix until evenly colored.
3. Pour the drained mandarin oranges into a bowl. Place a spoon in the bowl.
4. Place the shredded cheese on a paper plate.
5. Plan time to model the steps for this project and a completed Butterfly Treat.

Steps to Follow

1. Children place a graham cracker on a paper plate. They use a dull plastic knife to spread green cream cheese on the graham cracker.
2. Children place two mandarin orange slices for the wings, as shown.
3. Then they place two shreds of cheese for antennae, as shown.
4. Children enjoy their Butterfly Treats!

 Parent Letter

Dear Parent(s) or Guardian(s),

Today we cooked in class. Your child helped prepare "Butterfly Treats." Besides having fun cooking and eating, the children practiced these skills:

- vocabulary development
- listening to and following directions
- using small motor skills

For our unit *The Rainforest*, we will send home a variety of new recipes. Each recipe will be one that your child has tried in class and is excited about. We hope you have an opportunity to try this recipe again with your child. Allowing your child to help you in the kitchen is a wonderful way to reinforce learning skills while creating family memories.

Butterfly Treats

Materials

- graham cracker squares
- cream cheese spread
- green food coloring
- mandarin orange slices
- shredded cheese
- dull knife
- can opener

Steps to Follow

1. Color the cream cheese with a few drops of green food coloring.
2. Help your child spread the cream cheese on the cracker.
3. Create a butterfly design using two orange slices for wings and two cheese shreds for antennae.
4. Enjoy your Butterfly Treats!

Name _____

Animal Shadows

Match. Draw a line.

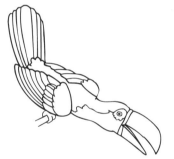

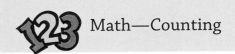 Math—Counting

Note: Children cut out and glue the numbers in the correct order.

Name _____

Counting Snake

Count. Cut. ✂ Glue. 🖊

9	3	6	10	2
1	5	8	7	4

Note: Children add the pictures and write the correct number.

Math—Beginning Computation

Name _____

Animal Addition

Count. Add. Write.

Working independently or in pairs, children play a memory match game with rainforest animal picture cards.

Materials

- page 157, laminated
- scissors
- sturdy envelope or folder

Animal Memory Match

Creating the Center

1. Laminate and cut apart page 157.
2. Plan time to model how the center is used.

Using the Center

1. Children place all the cards facedown on the table or floor.
2. The first player turns over two cards, looking for a match. If the cards match, the player keeps them. If the cards do not match, the player turns the cards facedown again.
3. The second player takes a turn and repeats the step above.
4. The game is played until all the cards are matched.

tree

tree frog

anaconda

anaconda

jaguar

jaguar

butterfly

butterfly

tree frog

tree frog

toucan

toucan

piranha

piranha

Animal Memory
Match

©2005 by Evan-Moor Corp.
All About the Rainforest • EMC 2408

Animal Memory
Match

©2005 by Evan-Moor Corp.
All About the Rainforest • EMC 2408

Animal Memory
Match

©2005 by Evan-Moor Corp.
All About the Rainforest • EMC 2408

Animal Memory
Match

©2005 by Evan-Moor Corp.
All About the Rainforest • EMC 2408

Animal Memory
Match

©2005 by Evan-Moor Corp.
All About the Rainforest • EMC 2408

Animal Memory
Match

©2005 by Evan-Moor Corp.
All About the Rainforest • EMC 2408

Animal Memory
Match

©2005 by Evan-Moor Corp.
All About the Rainforest • EMC 2408

Animal Memory
Match

©2005 by Evan-Moor Corp.
All About the Rainforest • EMC 2408

Animal Memory
Match

©2005 by Evan-Moor Corp.
All About the Rainforest • EMC 2408

Animal Memory
Match

©2005 by Evan-Moor Corp.
All About the Rainforest • EMC 2408

Animal Memory
Match

©2005 by Evan-Moor Corp.
All About the Rainforest • EMC 2408

Animal Memory
Match

©2005 by Evan-Moor Corp.
All About the Rainforest • EMC 2408

Children play a counting game in which they are tree frogs leaping from tree to tree.

Materials

- page 160, reproduced, one per child
- 12" x 18" (30.5 x 45.5 cm) green construction paper
- crayons
- scissors
- glue
- tape
- sidewalk chalk

Leaping Tree Frogs!

Preparation

1. Cut green construction paper lengthwise into four strips. Each child will need two strips to make a headband.
2. Draw 11 circles on the blacktop with sidewalk chalk and number them 10 through 20. These will be "trees."

Steps to Follow

1. Children take two strips of paper and bring them to an adult to assemble a headband. Tape the pieces together.
2. Then they color, cut out, and glue the tree frog head and feet to their headband.
3. Once the glue dries, children go outside and begin their outdoor activity.

How to Play

1. Children wear their tree frog headbands while playing this game.
2. Children take turns leaping from tree to tree in numerical order. They call out each number as they do this.

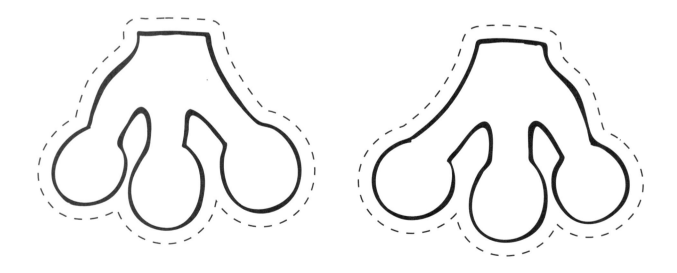

Music/Dramatic Play Activity

Rainforest Workers

I've been working in the rainforest,
Among the tall trees.
I've been working in the rainforest,
With the butterflies and bees.
Bats, parrots, and toucans,
So many different monkeys
All talking and swinging
Through the rainforest trees!

Monkeys, won't you swing,
Monkeys, won't you swing,
Monkeys, won't you swing
from the tree-ee-ees?
Monkeys, won't you swing,
Monkeys, won't you swing,
Monkeys, won't you swing
from the trees?

Animals live in the rain-forest.
Plants live in the rain-forest.
Animals and plants live in the rain-forest.
They need each other to live!

—*Gabe & Lisa Mathews*

Rainforest Family

Children learn about some of the people
who live and work in rainforests.

Rainforest Family

Our family lives in the rainforest.
The rainforest takes care of us.

In the rainforest, we hunt and fish.

2

In the rainforest, we pick fruit and nuts.

In the rainforest, we plant seeds in a garden.

In the rainforest, we play
with our pet monkey.

In the rainforest, we make
our home from trees.

In the rainforest, we live with our tribe.

Our family lives in the rainforest.
The rainforest takes care of us.

8

The End

Note: Teachers will make copies and cut in half for minibooks.

Reproducible Story

Rainforest Family

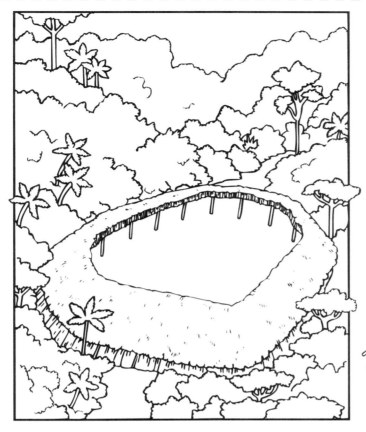

Our family lives in
the rainforest.
The rainforest
takes care of us.

1

In the rainforest,
we hunt and fish.

2

In the rainforest, we
pick fruit and nuts.

3

In the rainforest, we plant seeds in a garden.

4

In the rainforest, we play with our pet monkey.

5

In the rainforest,
we make our
home from trees.

6

In the rainforest,
we live with
our tribe.

7

Our family lives in
the rainforest.
The rainforest
takes care of us.

8

The End

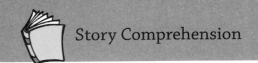 Story Comprehension

Note: Children draw a line from the people to the item they are pictured with in the Rainforest Family story.

Name _____

Rainforest Family

Match. Draw a line.

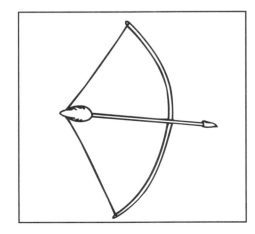

Note: See page 9 for suggestions for using the storyboard pieces on pages 179 and 181 for Rainforest Family.

Storyboard Pieces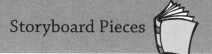

Rainforest Family

Rainforest Family

Rainforest Family

Rainforest Family

Rainforest Family

Rainforest Family

Rainforest Armbands

Children create two colorful "feathered" armbands.

Materials

- feather pattern below, reproduced several times per child
- armband-sized strips of construction paper, one per child
- yarn
- glue
- crayons or markers
- hole punch
- hole-reinforcer stickers, two per armband

Preparation

1. Cut construction paper into armband-sized strips. Punch a hole at each end of the armband and place a hole-reinforcer sticker around both holes.

2. Reproduce the feather pattern below several times for each child.

3. Cut two pieces of yarn and tie a knot at one end of each for each child's armband.

4. Explain to children that people of the rainforest use the materials around them to make useful and beautiful things. Tell children that sometimes people who live in the rainforest use colorful feathers to decorate masks or armbands.

Steps to Follow

1. Children take an armband with holes punched in the ends.

2. They color, cut out, and glue several feathers to their armbands.

3. Then children pull yarn through the holes at each end of the armband. An adult places the armband around the child's arm, tying the yarn into a bow.

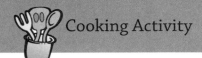

Cooking Activity

Note: Check for allergies before beginning any cooking activity. An allergic reaction can occur through taste, smell, or contact with allergens.

Explain to children that some people who live in the rainforest carry their lunch to school wrapped in a banana leaf. This leafy snack gives children a little "taste" of what that's like.

Leafy Wraps

Preparation

1. Prepare a cooking center with all materials assembled.
2. Set out the cream cheese to soften.
3. Model the steps for this cooking activity and a completed Leafy Wrap.

Steps to Follow

1. Children take a paper plate and a lettuce leaf.
2. They place a slice of turkey on the lettuce leaf.
3. Then they use a dull knife to spread cream cheese on the turkey.
4. Children fold the lettuce into a tight roll and secure it with a toothpick.
5. Then children remove the toothpick and enjoy their leafy snack.

Materials

- lettuce leaf washed and dried, one per wrap
- turkey lunchmeat, ½ slice per wrap
- cream cheese
- toothpicks
- dull knife
- paper plates
- paper towels

Dear Parent(s) or Guardian(s),

Today we cooked in class. Your child helped prepare "Leafy Wraps." Your child learned that some people who live in the rainforest carry their lunch to school wrapped in a banana leaf. Besides having fun cooking and eating, the children practiced these skills:

- listening to and following directions
- vocabulary and concept development
- using small motor skills

For our unit *The Rainforest*, we will send home a variety of new recipes. Each recipe will be one that your child has tried in class and is excited about. We hope you have an opportunity to try this recipe again with your child. Allowing your child to help you in the kitchen is a wonderful way to reinforce learning skills while creating family memories.

Leafy Wraps

Materials

- lettuce leaf, one per wrap
- turkey lunchmeat, ½ slice per wrap
- cream cheese
- toothpicks
- dull knife
- paper plates
- paper towels

Steps to Follow

1. Wash the lettuce leaves and pat them dry.
2. Take a paper plate and a lettuce leaf.
3. Place a slice of turkey on the lettuce leaf.
4. Use a dull knife to spread softened cream cheese on the turkey.
5. Fold the lettuce into a tight roll and secure it with a toothpick.
6. Remove the toothpick and enjoy your Leafy Wrap!

Note: People who study the plants and animals in the rainforest are called scientists. Children draw a line from each animal or thing to the scientist who studies it.

Name _____

Rainforest Scientists

Match. Draw a line.

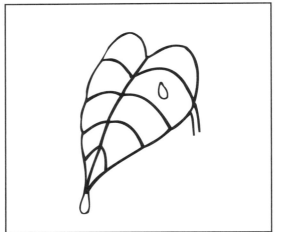

Note: Children count the items in each box and write the number in the space provided.

Math—Counting

Name _____

It's Fun to Count!

Look at the pictures in each row.

Count how many items are in each box. Write the number.

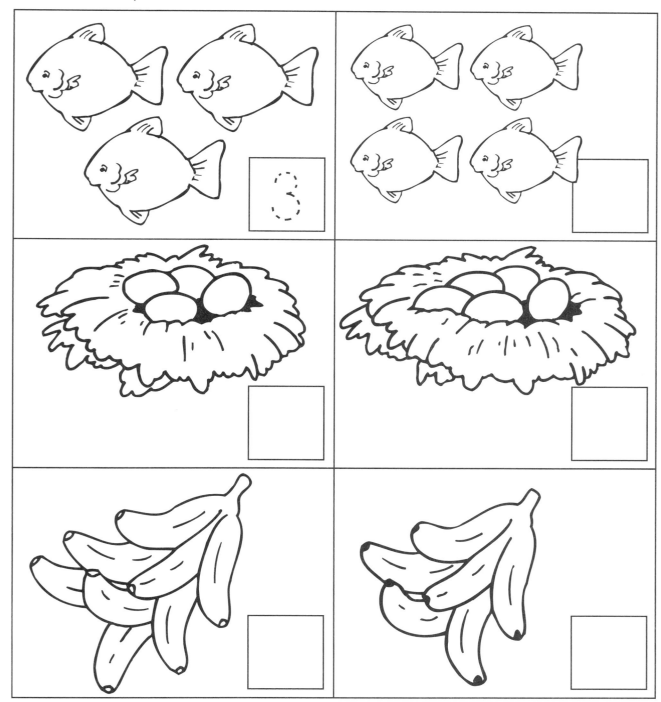

Butterfly Shapes

Creating the Center

1. Laminate and cut apart page 189.
2. Store the butterfly cards in a sturdy folder or envelope.
3. Reproduce the butterfly record sheet below. Keep a supply at the center.
4. Post a color chart and a shape chart at the center. Review the names of the geometric shapes and colors with children.
5. Plan time to model how the center is used.

Using the Center

1. Children choose a butterfly card and take a butterfly record sheet. Then they write the number of the butterfly card in the box on their record sheet.
2. Children color the butterfly record sheet to match the butterfly card they chose.

Children color the butterfly below to match the center card they chose.

Materials

- page 188, reproduced
- page 189, laminated
- scissors
- a sturdy folder or envelope
- crayons

Note: Reproduce this record sheet to use with Butterfly Shapes center activity.

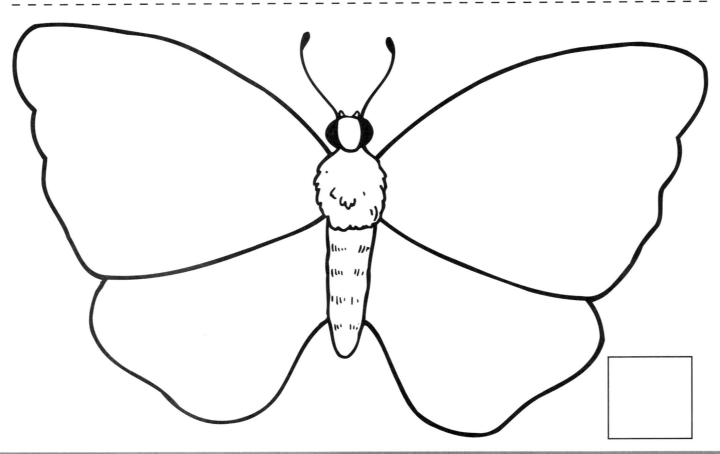

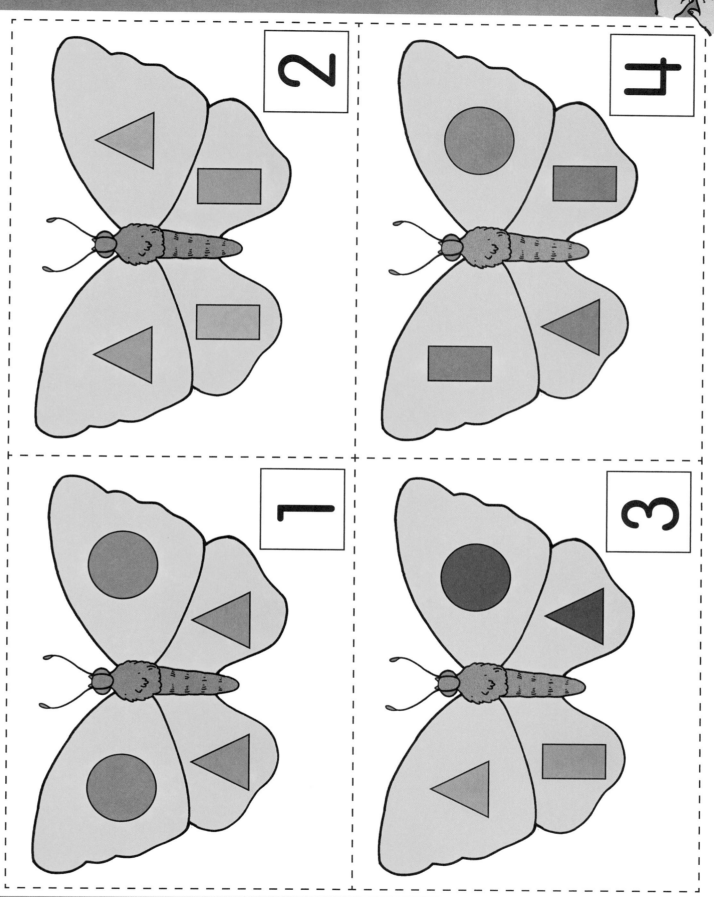

Butterfly Shapes

©2005 by Evan-Moor Corp.
All About the Rainforest • EMC 2408

Butterfly Shapes

©2005 by Evan-Moor Corp.
All About the Rainforest • EMC 2408

Butterfly Shapes

©2005 by Evan-Moor Corp.
All About the Rainforest • EMC 2408

Butterfly Shapes

©2005 by Evan-Moor Corp.
All About the Rainforest • EMC 2408

Note: Sing this song to the tune of "Skip to My Lou." In the second verse, children fill in the blank with the name of a rainforest animal or plant.

Music/Dramatic Play Activity

Study the Rainforest

Study the rainforest, that's what we do.

Study the plants and the animals, too.

Study the rainforest, that's what we do.

Study the rainforest—you can, too!

Learn about _____, that's what we do.

Learn about _____, that's what we do.

Learn about _____, that's what we do.

Learn about _____ —you can, too!

Care for the rainforest, that's what we do.

Care for the plants and the animals, too.

Care for the rainforest, that's what we do.

Care for the rainforest—you can, too!

Alphabet Cards

Use these colorful Alphabet Cards in a variety of ways. Simply laminate and cut apart the cards and store them in a sturdy envelope or box.

Alphabet cards can be used to practice skills such as:

- letter recognition
- letter-sound association
- visual perception

Alphabet Card Games ....

What's My Name?	Use the alphabet cards to introduce the names of the letters, both uppercase and lowercase.
Make a Match	Children match a lowercase and uppercase letter. They then turn the cards over to self-check. If a correct match has been made, the child will see a picture of the same object whose name begins with the letter being matched.
First-Sound Game	Use the alphabet cards as phonics flash cards and ask children to identify the sound of each letter.
ABC Order	Children take all of the uppercase or lowercase cards and place them in alphabetical order.

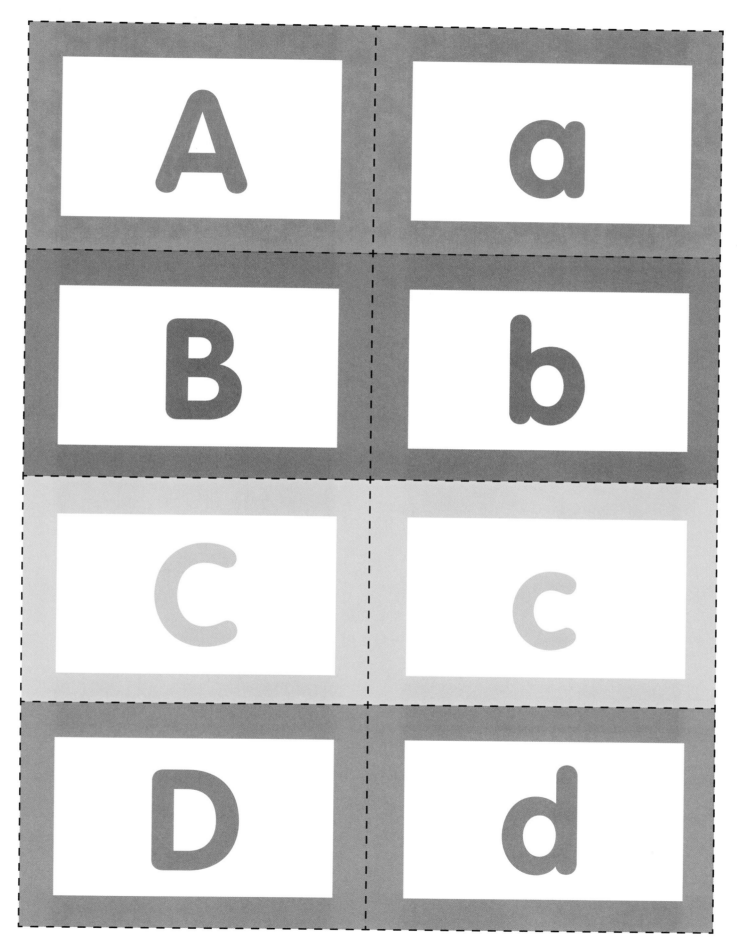

ant

Ant

bat

Bat

capybara

Capybara

duck

Duck

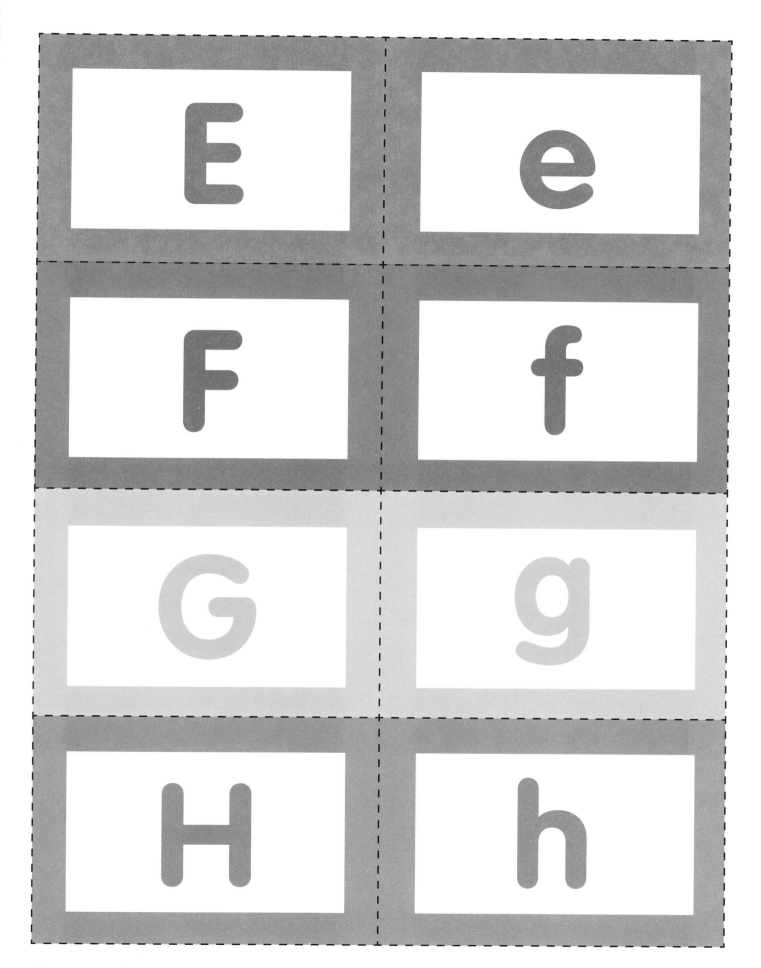

eagle

Eagle

frog

Frog

guava

Guava

hummingbird

Hummingbird

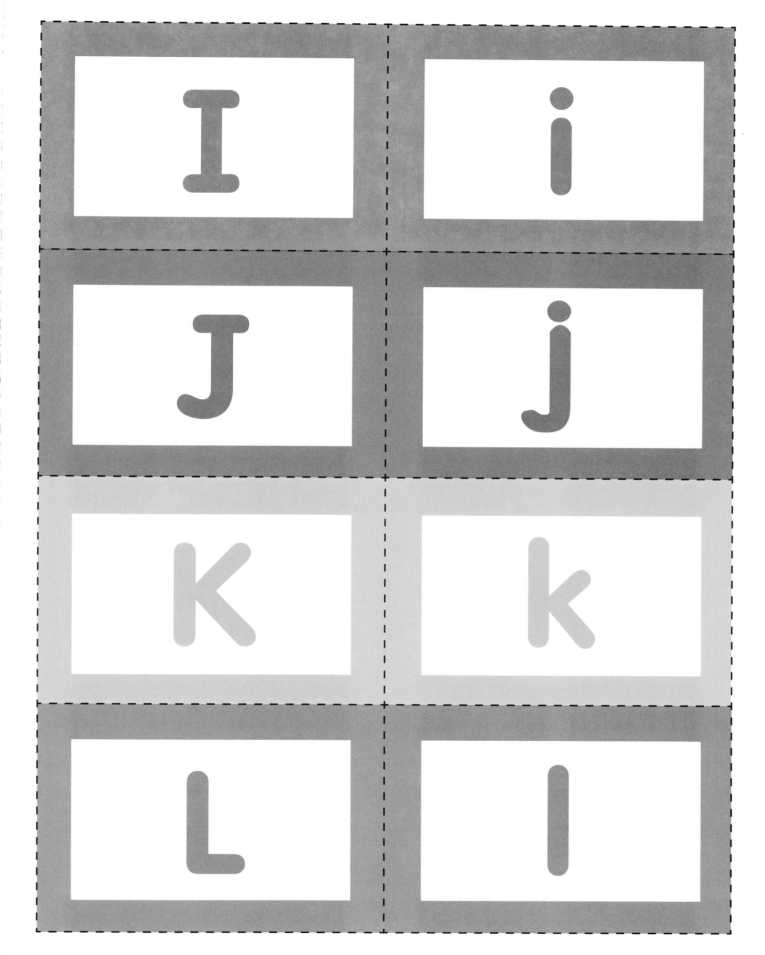

insects

Insects

jaguar

Jaguar

kiwi

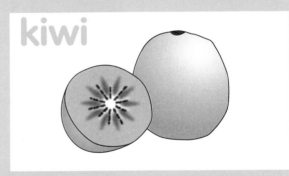

Kiwi

log

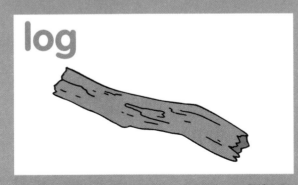

Log

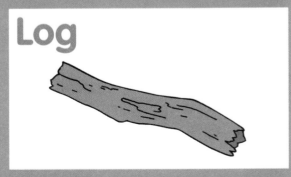

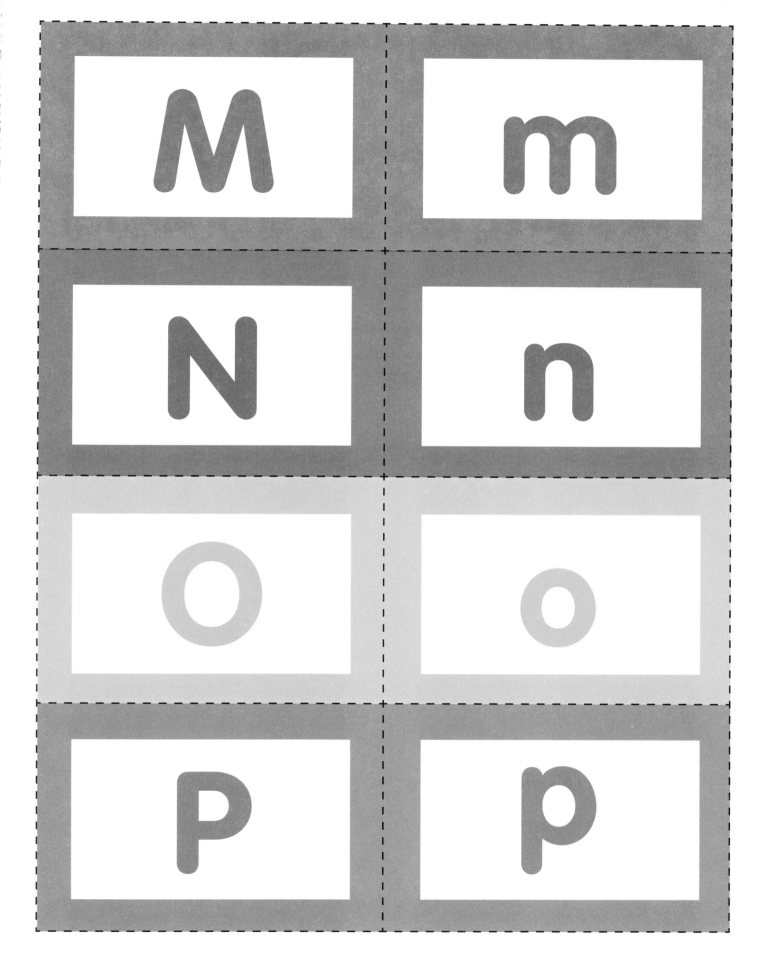

monkey

Monkey

nuts

Nuts

orange

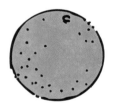

Orange

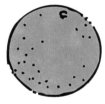

piranha

Piranha

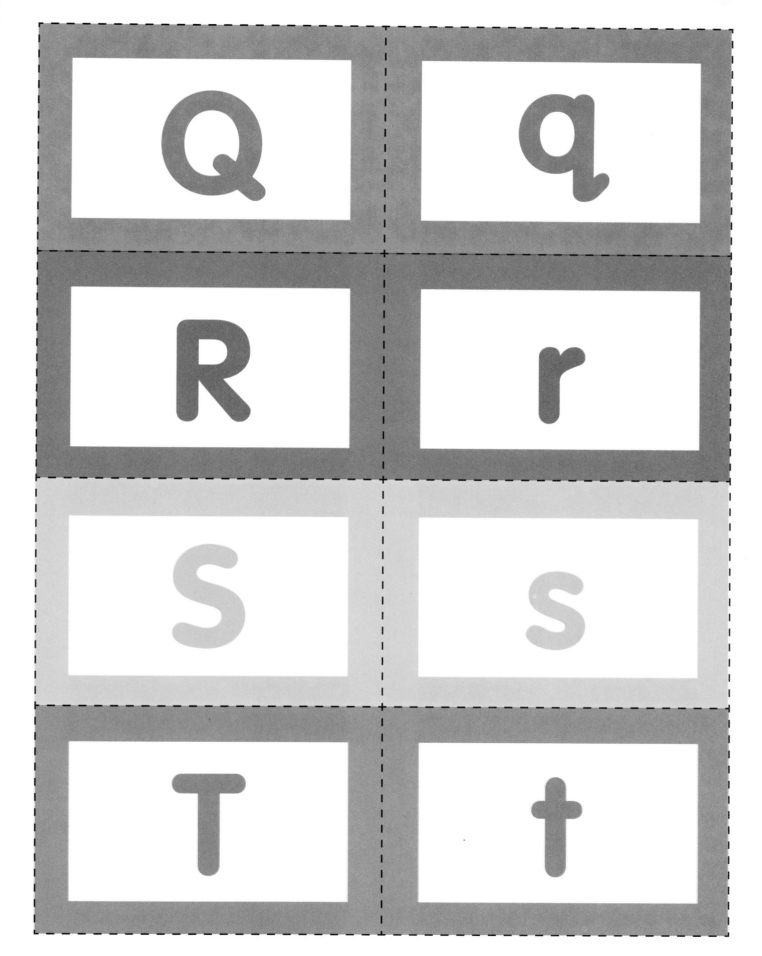

quiet

shhh!!

Quiet

shhh!!

rain

Rain

sloth

Sloth

toucan

Toucan

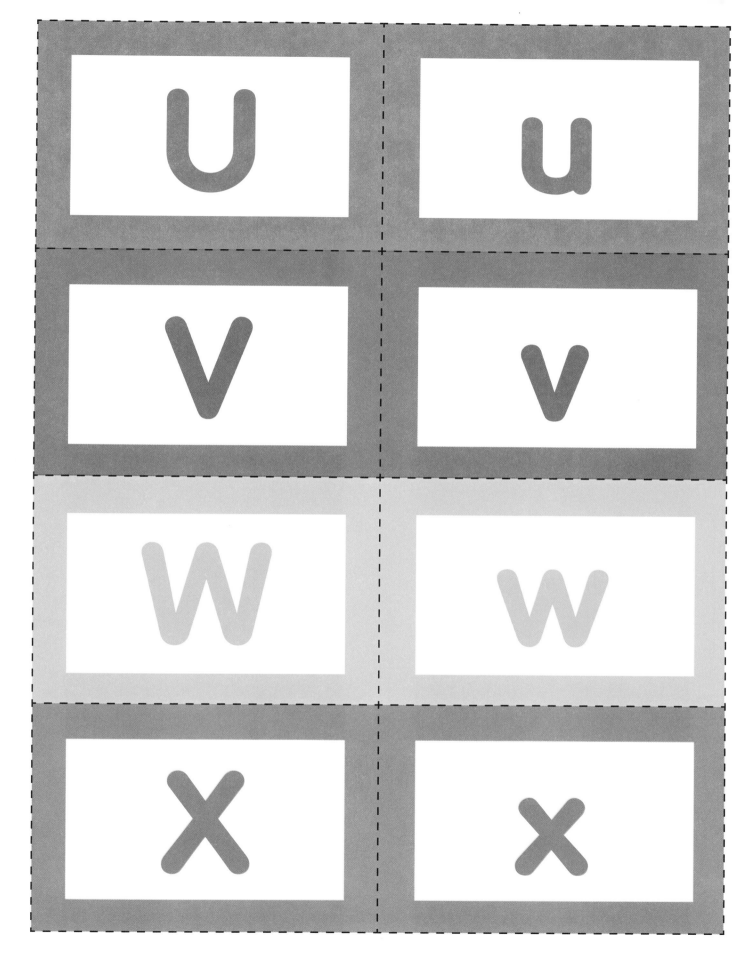

understory

Understory

vines

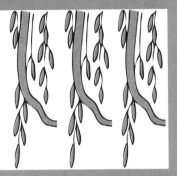

Vines

water

Water

x

X

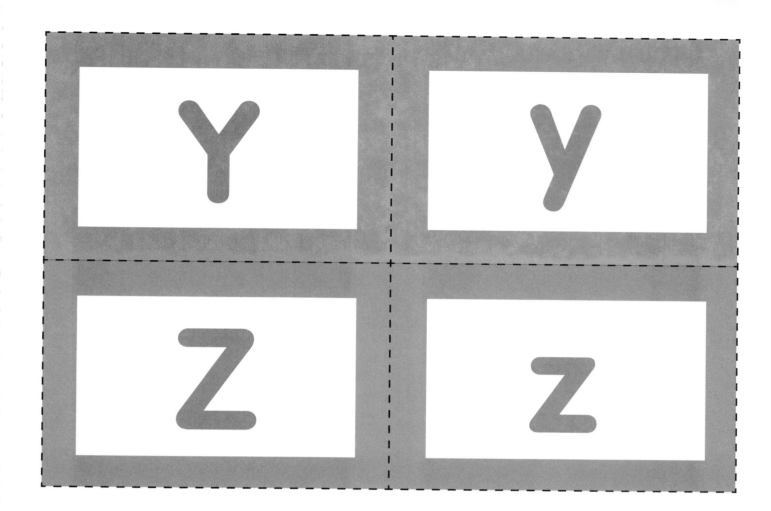

yellow bananas

Yellow bananas

zoologist

Zoologist

Answer Key

Page 28

Page 41

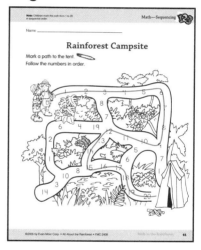

Page 42

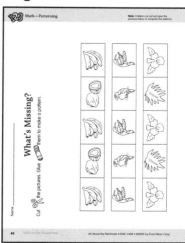

Page 46

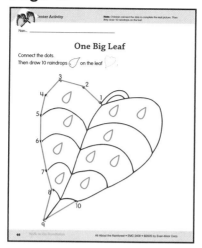

Page 66

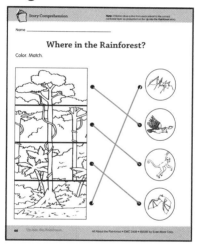

Page 77

Page 106

Page 115

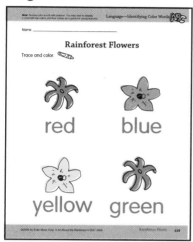

Page 116

Page 117

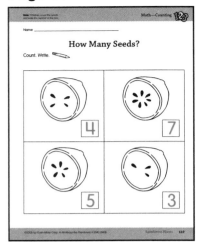

Page 142

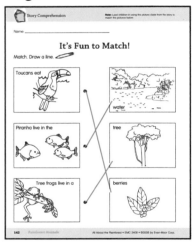

Page 153

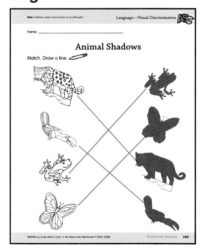

Page 154

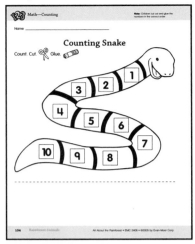

Page 155

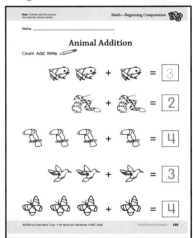

Page 178

Page 186

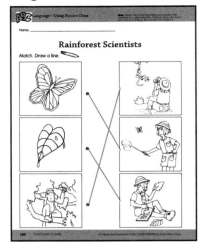

Page 187

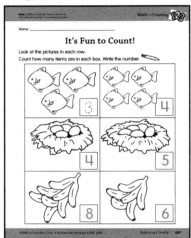